“Exploring Computer Systems: From Fundamentals to Advanced Concepts”

GoodMan, Volume 1

Patrick Mukosha

Published by Patrick Mukosha, 2023.

Also by Patrick Mukosha

GoodMan
Resilient Strategies: Thriving in Harsh Business Conditions
Strategic Entrepreneurship: Navigating The Path To Success
Decisive Power: Navigating How to Make Toughest Decisions
Unraveling Information Systems: Exploring the Core Concepts
"Reigning the Boardroom: A Trailblazing Guide to Corporate Governance Success"
Fortifying Digital Fortress: A Comprehensive Guide to Information Systems Security
"Unleashing the Power of Inclusive Innovation: Transforming the World for All"
"Exploring Computer Systems: From Fundamentals to Advanced Concepts"

Dedication

The author is indebted to a large number of researchers, and consultants in the field of Information and Communication Technologies (ICT), whose works were referred to in writing this book – and appears below and in the bibliography.

The author also would like to acknowledge the encouragement of my wife; Gracious Lumba Maboshe-Mukosha, my special colleagues Bernard Chisanga (MHSRIP), Amos Wambili and my children, whose comments and constructive criticism kept the author alive. The author also benefitted from the comments of many colleagues: Paul Wilson and Peter Bird. They generously shared their insights and experiences in an evolving field where tacit knowledge is indispensable.

The author wishes to thank his late Father; Isaac Mulando Mukosha (MHSRIP) and late mother; Rebecca Mukosha (MHSRIP), for their endless love.

Special thanks go to Lionel Hugh Weston; my former Secondary School Teacher and Guardian, without whom I would never have had a strong education foundation in life. His contribution in my education career is immeasurable. I shall forever remain indebted to him and the entire Weston's family.

“Exploring Computer Systems:

From Fundamentals to Advanced Concepts”

Copyright Notice

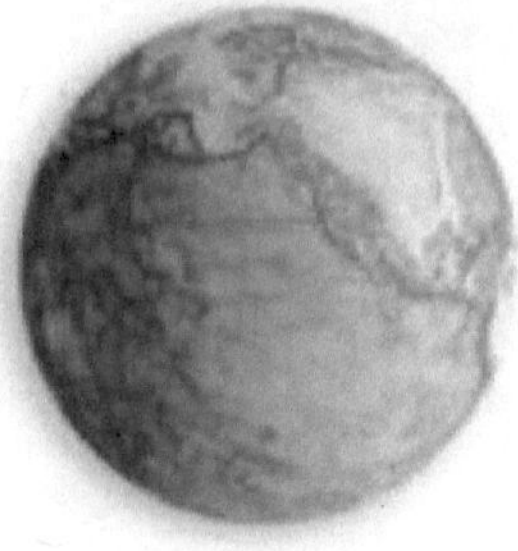

First published: August, 2023

Publisher: Patrick Mukosha PhD

Trademarks

All terms mentioned in this book that are known to be trademarks or service marks have been appropriately capitalized. The Author and the publisher cannot attest to the accuracy of this information. Use of a term in this book should not be regarded as affecting the validity of any trademark or service mark.

Warning and Disclaimer

Every effort has been made to make this book as complete and as accurate as possible, but no warranty or fitness is implied. The information provided in this book is on as is basis. The Author and the Publisher shall have neither liability nor responsibility to any person or entity with respect to any loss or damage arising from the use the information contained in this book.

Author: Patrick Chisenga Mukosha PhD

Abstract

The essential manual "Exploring Computer Systems: *From Fundamentals to Advanced Concepts*" takes readers on a thorough tour of the world of computer systems. This book offers a thorough examination of computer systems, starting with the fundamentals and advancing to complex concepts.

The book's excellent basis in computer architecture and components at the outset makes it understandable for both newcomers and seasoned IT experts. The basic concepts of hardware, software, and their relationships are covered, enabling readers to comprehend how contemporary computer systems operate within.

Readers delve into the complexities of operating systems, including as process management, memory management, and file systems, as they move through the chapters. The author is succinct and straightforward. These complicated subjects are demystified by the author's succinct and simple explanations, making them understandable to readers of all skill levels.

This book's covering on networking and communication protocols is one of its best qualities. It offers a thorough review of computer networking and communication in local and wide-area networks, illuminating terms like TCP/IP, routing, and security. The fascinating worlds of virtualization and cloud computing are also highlighted in the book. The impact of virtual machines and cloud services, which have transformed the IT environment and increased computing flexibility, scalability, and affordability, is explained to readers.

Chapter 1: Introduction to Computer Systems

1.1. What are Computer Systems?

A computer system is a sophisticated, interconnected configuration of hardware, software, and data that is used to effectively carry out a variety of operations and procedures. It is made up of various parts that operate harmoniously together to process information, resolve issues, and carry out orders. Virtually every part of modern life, from home computers to huge data centres, depends on computer systems.

Hardware and software are the two fundamental components of a computer system. These components work together to carry out a variety of tasks, from straightforward calculations to complex simulations. Let's examine these elements in more detail:

1.1.1. Hardware Components:

Computer hardware includes all of the tangible parts and devices that go into building a computer system. These elements consist of:

- **The CPU** - The central processing unit (CPU), also known as the "brain" of the computer, is in charge of carrying out calculations, carrying out orders, and controlling data flow.
- **Random Access Memory (RAM):** RAM offers quick and temporary storage for information and commands that the CPU is actively using. It enables easy access to and manipulation of data.
- **Storage Devices**: Even when a computer is off, these devices continue to save data. Solid State Drives (SSDs) and Hard Disk Drives (HDDs) are two examples of long-term storage devices.
- **Devices for Input and Output**: These tools allow communication between the user and the computer. Keyboards, mouse, and touchscreens are often used input devices, whereas displays, printers, and speakers are frequently used output devices.
- **Motherboard:** CPU, memory, and storage devices are all connected to and communicate with one another via the motherboard, which serves as the main circuit board.
- **Expansion Cards**: These cards, like graphics cards, network interface cards, and sound cards, give the computer system additional capabilities.

1.1.2. Software Components: The set of instructions and programs used by computers to complete specific tasks are referred to as software.

Software falls into two primary categories:

- **System Software**: consists of the operating system (OS), which controls hardware resources, presents a user interface, and permits the execution of software programs. The operating systems Windows, macOS, Linux, and Android are a few examples.
- **Application Software**: These are programs created to carry out certain functions or deliver particular services. Word processors, web browsers, and other software are examples.

The compatibility of a computer system's hardware and software components determines how well it functions. The physical resources and computational power are provided by the hardware, while the interfaces and instructions for efficiently using these resources are provided by the software.

Thus, a computer system is a dynamic collection of hardware and software that collaborates to process data, carry out tasks, and provide users with useful results. The development of computer systems has transformed a variety of fields and our ability to communicate and solve problems, influencing how we live and work in the digital age.

1.1. Evolution and History of Computer Systems

The intriguing history of computer systems over the years has had a profound impact on how far humanity has come. The history of computers is characterized by inventions, breakthroughs, and the relentless efforts of visionaries and engineers. Computer systems have evolved from their simple beginnings as mechanical calculators to the sophisticated digital wonders we have today. An overview of the significant turning points in the development of computer systems is given in this section.

The Earliest Calculators:

1.1.1. Abacus (3000 BCE):

One of the earliest known tools for calculating is the abacus, a straightforward counting instrument. It was made of stones or beads strung on a rod, with each row signifying a distinct place value. Second-century BCE Antikythera Mechanism the Antikythera Mechanism, a prehistoric Greek analog computer, was used to forecast astronomical locations and eclipses. One of the oldest examples of mechanical computation, so to speak.

1.1.2. Mechanical Calculators:

Pascal's Calculator (1642): Blaise Pascal invented the mechanical calculator, which used a set of gears and wheels to add and subtract integers.

1.1.3. Emergence of Digital Computers

One of the first general-purpose electronic computers was the ENIAC (1945), also known as the Electronic Numerical Integrator and Computer. It could do a wide range of calculations and was enormous in size.

UNIVAC I (1951): The UNIVAC I was the first commercially available computer and was employed in a variety of fields, including business, science, and the military.

1.1.4. Transistors And Microprocessors Are Introduced:

- **Transistors (1947):** By offering a more dependable and effective method of controlling electrical impulses, the transistor changed computing. This signalled the change from vacuum tubes to more compact and quick components.
- **Microprocessors (1971):** The creation of the microprocessor by Intel (Intel 4004) and later generations resulted in the shrinking of processing capacity, enabling the integration of sophisticated circuitry onto a device in 1971.
- **Babbage's Analytical Engine (1837):** Charles Babbage developed the idea for the Analytical Engine, which featured a memory, a control flow, and an arithmetic logic unit. Although it was never built, it served as the model for contemporary computers.

1. **Digital Revolution and Personal Computers:**

The Altair 8800, which was first made available as a kit in 1975, is one of the earliest personal computers. Due to its popularity, enthusiasts developed hardware and software for their own purposes.

The personal computer era officially began in 1981 with the release of the IBM PC. Due to its open architecture, other vendors were able to produce compatible software.

1.1.6. Internet And Networking:

The Advanced Research Projects Agency (ARPA), a division of the United States Department of Defence, created the ARPANET network in 1969, which served as the forerunner of the current internet.

1.1.7. **World Wide Web (1989):** Tim Berners-Lee's development of the World Wide Web made the internet a user-friendly platform for information sharing and accessing worldwide.

1.1.8. Beyond Mobile Computing:

Tablets and smartphones (2000s): Because of the widespread use of smartphones and tablets, computing power is now accessible to us on the go for communication, entertainment, and productivity.

1.1.9. **Cloud computing and IoT:** The Internet of Things (IoT) changed communication by enabling the interconnection of common things. Scalable and distant access to computational and data storage resources was made possible by cloud computing.

The constant pursuit of technological progress and the urge for innovation among humans are reflected in the evolution of computer systems. Computer systems have transformed from mechanical gadgets to potent digital ecosystems, becoming an essential component of contemporary civilization and affecting industry, communication, and how people view and engage with the outside world. Future developments are expected to be much more notable, driven by cutting-edge technologies like quantum computing, artificial intelligence, and biotechnology.

1.2. Basic Components of a Computer System

A computer system is a sophisticated collection of connected parts that collaborate to process data and carry out various activities. Gaining an understanding of how computer systems work and interact requires an understanding of their fundamental parts. The basic parts of a computer system are described in general in this section.

1.2.1. CPU, Or Central Processing Unit:

The CPU, often known as the central processing unit, is the brains of the computer system. It is in charge of carrying out calculations and carrying out orders. Clock cycles and gigahertz (GHz) are units used to describe the CPU's performance and speed. There are two primary units in it:

- **Control Unit:** Instructions are managed by the control unit, which retrieves them from memory and converts them into signals that other parts can comprehend.
- **ALU, or Arithmetic Logic Unit**: performs the addition, subtraction, multiplication, and division calculations as well as the logical operations AND, OR, and NOT required for data processing.

1. **Memory Hierarchy**:

The memory hierarchy refers to the various levels of memory that computer systems have, each with a different speed and capacity. The quickest and smallest memory components, registers are used to store the data and instructions that the CPU is currently processing.

- **Memory Cache:** Cache memory, which can store frequently accessed data faster than main memory (RAM), shortens the time the CPU must wait for data retrieval.
- **Main Memory (RAM):** Offers momentary storage for information and commands that the CPU is actively using. RAM is volatile, which means that when the computer is turned off, its contents are gone.
- **Secondary Storage**: Non-volatile storage components like Solid State Drives (SSDs) and Hard Disk Drives (HDDs) can keep data safe even while the computer is not running.

1. **Devices for Input and Output:**

Users can enter data and commands into the computer system using input devices, while output devices show or provide results:

- **Keyboard:** Used to enter instructions and text.
- **Mouse:** Objects on the screen can be pointed at and selected using the mouse.
- **Touchscreen**: Enables close engagement with the display.
- **Monitor:** Shows visual results.
- **Printer:** Prints papers on paper using a printer.
- **Speaker:** Audio sound is produced by the speaker.

1.1.4 **Motherboard:** The computer system's main circuit board, the motherboard links and enables communication between other parts. It includes:

- **CPU Socket**: The CPU is held in place by the CPU socket, which also connects it to the rest of the system.

- **RAM Slots**: Memory modules are put into RAM slots.
- **Expansion Slots**: Enable the addition of extra components, such as graphics cards.
- **Input / Output Ports**: Connect external devices like USB, HDMI, and Ethernet to the input/output ports.

1.1.5 **Power Supply and Cooling System**: The power supply unit (PSU), which transforms AC electricity from a wall socket into DC power needed by computer components, is a component of the power supply system. By dissipating the heat produced during operation, the cooling system, which includes fans and heat sinks, prevents overheating.

The basis for understanding how a computer system functions is an understanding of these fundamental parts. Each component has a specific function that contributes to the overall functionality, and when these components work together, operations like executing apps and processing data are carried out without any hiccups. These elements will stay essential to the foundation of computer systems as computer technology develops while incorporating new developments.

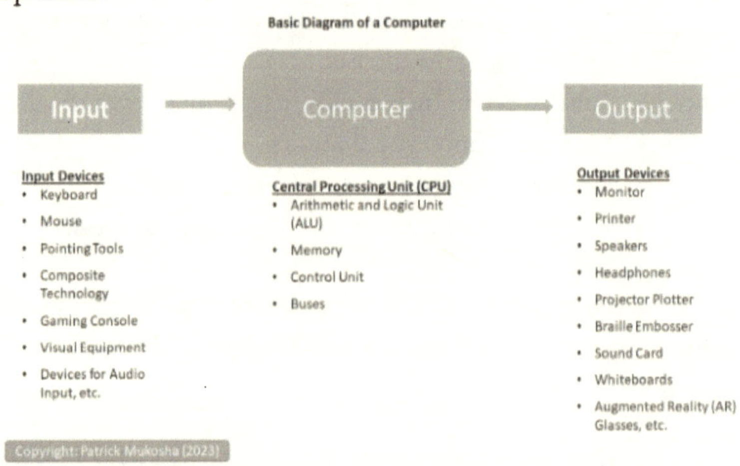

Figure 1: Basic Diagram of a Computer

Note: Modern computers are built on what is known as the "von Neumann architecture," a fundamental computer concept. John von Neumann, a mathematician and computer scientist, created this architecture in the 1940s. It is made up of a number of essential parts that work together to process and store data.

1.3. Role and Importance of Computer Systems in Modern Society

Today, computers are a need. An extremely efficient information system has been developed by computers to aid in streamlining organizational management. As a result, it is a crucial instrument for every sector of society, including commerce, banking, government, entertainment, daily life, industry, and administration. All significant businesses, whether departmental, governmental, or private, can be said to use computers for a range of daily tasks, and the computer industry is currently one of the fastest-growing in the world.

A number of small computers and one or more major computer systems are typically present in each organization. While many little microcomputers are used for word processing, the system is a superb machine for data processing jobs. Our lives now depend on computers in some way. Computer usage may often be broken down into various categories. It is well known that computer usage time is increasing quickly.

Computers have been used to start businesses everywhere:

1.3.1. **Computers' Place in Business** - Computer use is one of the most prevalent in the corporate world. In fact, due to the availability of extremely affordable microcomputers, small enterprises also use computers. Business enterprises must today process a large number of information and numbers. So many firms now use computers for a variety of tasks, including compensation calculation, inventory tracking, issuing and receiving business statements, mailings, and invoices, and more.

The management of office automation and the use of computers and office technology to aid other managers, clerks, and other employees. One of them is a word processing-style electronic method that allows us to quickly write and edit letters, reports, documents, and other types of work. Many of the office's typical letters, including those for invites, payment of the balance, and other purposes. Additionally, regional business associations employ computers to design, store, and dispatch envoys to certain locations. The benefits of employing computers in this area are undoubtedly crucial in a company setting.

1.3.2. **Computers' Place in Education** - As science and technology improve, the computer may eventually replace books in bookstores as a means of disseminating information to the general population. In other words, the computer will alter how we acquire knowledge and how we retain it. A computer can be used to implement administration-related tasks such student registration, class scheduling, processing test results, and teachers' and students' personal storage quickly and efficiently. Exam results processing has been automated recently. The IPT is also responsible for analysing scientific research findings, automating office tasks, and using computers. In actuality, computer use is similar to cataloguing books in libraries. Last but not least, computer-assisted education is used for teaching and learning processes not only at institutions of higher learning but also in schools. It is strongly emphasized that in the field of education, research is what is important is the ease and help students and teachers in the teaching and learning.

1.3.3. **The Role of Computers in Banking and Finance** - The operating budget of an institution includes data from savings accounts, fixed deposits, loans, investments, profitability analysis, and other financial transactions. Standard and repeated measures are employed. With that, the financial institution becomes the first user to recognize the value of computers in terms of time savings. Employing financial institutions, such as electronic fund transfers, is common. For instance, every bank branch nationwide has a terminal, as do stores like supermarkets and gas stations and workplaces like factories and hotels. By entering employee identification numbers, the business transfers employee salaries into accounts, which are subsequently used to make purchases at petrol stations, motels, and supermarkets.

The term "money transfer facility" refers to the electronic transfer of money, which is a highly efficient, secure, and efficient way to conduct financial operations. An individual can issue, transfer, and add cash or checks to the current balance at any moment using the ETC facility. The primary goal of using computers in financial institutions is undoubtedly to help clients organize their affairs and provide services better and more efficiently, reduce financial transaction fraud, and eliminate community cash transactions in order to establish a cashless society.

1.3.4. **Computers' Place in Law** - Recent years have seen the usage of computers in the legislative process. The creation of documents with a word processor is the most crucial use. The use of computer accounting legislation also involves processing to create weekly and monthly reports, keep track of payments consulting, a journal for the most recent legal information for consumers regarding the various court procedures, as well as to keep track of users.

Due to the complexity of this subject, it is necessary to locate the necessary data, whether it be from a law journal, a significant case, a scale, statistics, or significant choices, in order to decide whether to keep the legal data bank. Thus, using a single computer will enable attorneys, aspiring attorneys, and law students to find pertinent information quickly and with better service.

1.3.5. Computers' Place in the Medical Sector - Computers are used in hospitals and clinics to keep patient information, schedule physicians, nurses, and other staff, inventory, and buy medications, conduct medical research, and make diagnoses. The use of information technology and computer-based technologies has aided medical professionals in disease diagnosis. It is obvious that computers are used in the medical industry to offer solutions to challenging issues. One of the newest computer technologies that helps people with disabilities.

People with impairments can communicate using a terminal to instruct a computer to carry out a vocal task thanks to microprocessor-based speech systems. The development of computers has also made it possible for the deaf and blind to communicate, whether via the use of a speech synthesizer or a keyboard. They may become more active as a result and be able to perform tasks they previously were unable to. In addition to typical data processing tasks including patient billing, medical statistics, staff scheduling, and other tasks, these tasks have been expedited and processed by computers.

A centralized patient database can house the hospital information system. In fact, a computer is designed to grow and analyse bacteria, viruses, and other infectious agents to automatically detect and identify a disease, allowing hospitals and laboratories to start treating. This is made possible by the use of information technology. For instance, the Computer Aided Demography (CAT) machine is utilized for the task. In a similar way, computers are used to monitor a patient's psychological factors including blood pressure, body temperature, and ECG (Electro-Cardiograph) and sound an alarm if anything out of the ordinary occurs.

The computer will read several variables and compare them to industry standards for this purpose. Doctors and nurses will be alerted by the computer to offer a warning if something unusual occurs. It was clearly discovered that the computer has several options for accommodations in the medical industry.

1.3.6. **Computers' Place in Industry** - The use of computers and the creation of human like robots are very beneficial to industry. For instance, industrial manufacturing requires a large number of computers to process data gathered from workers, clients, sales, product information, production schedules, and other sources. Yes, the computer used to direct the manufacturing process replied.

The production of information processing inventory control, in particular, keeps track of the most recent data regarding the remaining inventory of raw materials and completed items that are used to calculate the value of inventory and stock status. This computer can notify the engaged employees when it is time to deliver finished goods to the customer and when to order the necessary raw materials. Similar to how information about an item's structure is stored, computers are also used in the material demand planning processes to speed up operations. The scope of appearing in the computer sector is enormous, and it also has an impact on how an economy develops.

1.3.7. **Computers' Place in Daily Life** - Home air conditioning, lighting, and safety are all controlled by microcomputers. The usage of computers at home enables housewives to access the most recent fashion information and place orders for supermarket items and videos. In addition to making an inventory at home and setting a budget. Everything here is related to a small computer that is linked to the national data bank. Computers can be used by kids to play educational games or learn academic material. However, it is evident that in our society, computers have evolved into informational machines.

1.3.8. **The Role Of Computers In Government** - The government is one of the sectors that uses computers the most to carry out administrative tasks. All the information required for planning and decision-making, including data on people, services, economic planning, and land development projects, may be acquired quickly. Long-term weather forecasting using a computer is now possible.

Due to faster and better information, there may be a greater chance of a fatality. The use of computers in the construction of spacecraft, clothing for astronauts, and flight schedules also contributed to the success of Neil Armstrong's lunar landing on July 23, 1969. This demonstrates the critical role computers play in space transportation. The use of computers simplified the collection of service tax and income tax. Keeping track of taxpayers is a chore that can be done more swiftly and efficiently using a computer than it can be done manually, which can cause a number of issues.

Similar to this, computer storage was used in the military before the war simulation appeared on the screen. Computers are also utilized to track the enemy's movements in border regions. By determining the direction of traffic utilizing the many detection techniques, traffic flow can be successfully managed. In this method, the computer will allow the green light to remain on for a reasonable amount of time if there are more vehicles coming from one direction. Computers can also be used for automobile registration and business owner tasks. A large portion of administrative tasks are managed by computers. This not only saves time, but also makes everything more useful.

1.3.9. **Computers' Place in Entertainment** - Now, it is possible to program the computer to play music. Computer-controlled music venues are more affordable and accessible at all times. The dance and music are also arranged using computers. Every game calls for movement. The greatest way to understand movement is through careful examination of a physical system.

High-quality graphics can also be displayed by computers with the right programming. The creation process is sped up when drawing on a computer. Compared to conventional narrative, the work of art can be completed and reviewed quickly. Computer-generated cartoon movies have become very popular.

In conclusion, the current pattern of life has altered as a result of the rapid advancement of science and technology. Everything that was previously processed, information gathered, or any part of the many domains was done manually, which carries a lot of risk and must be made more effective, quicker, and more useful with the use of information technology or computers. Covering the use in numerous industries, including business, finance, industry, education, government, and other disciplines have the goal to actualize each nation's development. Computers are now indisputably at the core and foundation of modern society. Regardless of the industry, a large number of people have embraced computing. In addition to aiding in calculations, information storage, and decision detection, it will also boost productivity and efficiency.

However, they claimed that it is now obvious that the use of computers has been widespread. The computer is a machine in the information age and also the major artery of all machinery administration in any sector, in keeping with globalization and the borderless world.

1.4. Facilitator of Communication and Information Exchange:

The ability to connect in real time when separated by great distances has changed communication. Instant messaging, email, social networking, and video conferencing are all made possible by computer networks that power the internet. This connectedness encourages international cooperation and communication by cutting across boundaries, cultures, and languages.

Computers have indeed revolutionized practically every aspect of modern life by simplifying communication and information sharing. The following are some significant ways that computers facilitate communication and information exchange:

1.4.1. **Email** - Email is a primary form of communication in both personal and professional settings, and computers make it possible to create, send, and receive emails. Email enables the quick international transmission of text, documents, and multimedia items.

1.4.2. **Instant Messaging and Chat:** Real-time text, phone, and video communication is made possible through computer-based instant messaging and chat programs like WhatsApp, Facebook Messenger, and Slack. Whether for social interactions or professional collaboration, these platforms provide rapid and effective communication.

1.4.3. **Social media:** Online social networks like Facebook, Twitter, and Instagram use computer technology to link individuals all over the world. These platforms enable communication and engagement by enabling individuals and organizations to share information, updates, and multimedia content.

1.4.4. **Video Conferencing**: Remote communication has been transformed by computers thanks to video conferencing software like Zoom, Skype, and Microsoft Teams. Face-to-face communication is made possible through these platforms, allowing for the conduct of virtual meetings, seminars, and interviews regardless of geographic location.

1.4.5. **File Sharing and Cloud Storage:** Using cloud storage services like Google Drive, Dropbox, and iCloud, computers make it simple to share and store documents, images, movies, and other digital assets. This simplifies information sharing between people and teams and promotes collaborative work.

1.4.6. **Online Communities and Forums:** Computers enable the establishment of and participation in online communities, forums, and message boards. These platforms make it possible for people with similar interests to communicate, seek guidance, and have in-depth conversations.

1.4.7. **Blogging and Content Creation:** Computers play a crucial role in the development of material, such as blogs, articles, videos, and podcasts. A global audience can access the knowledge and opinions of people and organizations through blogging platforms and content management systems (CMS).

1.4.8. **E-commerce:** E-commerce platforms use computers to let buyers and sellers share information and conduct transactions. Customers can shop online, read product reviews and details, and browse products.

1.4.9. **Technology in Education:** By enabling online study and remote education, computers have transformed education. Students and teachers can access course materials, assignments, and feedback thanks to learning management systems (LMS) and educational software.

1.4.10. **Government and Public Service:** Computers are used by governments to deliver online services including tax filing, permit applications, and information dissemination. This improves citizen engagement and streamlines government operations.

1.4.11. **Healthcare Information Systems**: Electronic health records (EHRs) and telemedicine rely on computers to securely store and communicate patient information, enabling doctor-patient communication and enhancing patient care.

1.4.12. **News and media:** The creation and distribution of news and media information depend on computers. Media companies and journalists may share information with a global audience thanks to online news platforms and digital publishing tools.

Thus, computers are now essential tools for exchanging information and facilitating communication in the current world. They have changed how we access, produce, and share information across many different spheres of life in addition to connecting people and organizations over great distances.

1.5. Economic Growth and Innovation Catalyst

Computer systems have accelerated economic growth in the corporate world through greater productivity, automation, and innovation. Computer systems are used in a variety of industries, including finance, healthcare, manufacturing, and entertainment, for tasks including data analysis, supply chain management, and consumer engagement.

Computers have fostered innovation and economic progress in many different ways. Their widespread economic integration has had a significant impact on productivity, efficiency, and the emergence of new industries. Here are some important things to think about:

1.5.1. **Increased Productivity:** Productivity has increased dramatically across industries thanks to computers. They can handle enormous volumes of data quickly, automate monotonous processes, and carry out intricate computations. Economic growth results from firms being able to generate more goods and services while using less resources.

1.5.2. **Creation of New Industries:** The advancement and widespread use of computers have resulted in the emergence of completely new markets and industries. Hardware, software, and IT services are all part of the technology sector, which is now a significant engine of economic expansion. Additionally, there are numerous sectors that depend on computers, like e-commerce, social media, app development, and online advertising.

1.5.3. **Innovation Accelerator:** Computers act as an innovation accelerator by offering tools for research, design, and experimentation. They allow researchers, engineers, and scientists to simulate experiments, model complicated systems, and evaluate data, resulting in advances in a variety of sectors like medicine, materials science, and environmental study.

1.5.4. **Globalization and Connectivity:** The internet and computers have linked the economies of different countries. They have facilitated worldwide supply chains, outsourcing, and international trade. This interconnection has facilitated economic progress by enabling companies to access wider markets and a more diversified pool of talent.

1.5.5. **Start-ups and Entrepreneurship**: The cost of computers and software tools has reduced the entry barrier for start-ups and entrepreneurship. Today, small groups or individuals can create novel goods and services, upending traditional markets and fostering economic dynamism.

1.5.6. **Data-Driven Decision Making:** The ability to gather, analyse, and analyse massive volumes of data has been made feasible by computers. Businesses and governments may now make better judgments, run their affairs more efficiently, and find fresh chances for expansion and efficiency.

1.5.7. **Education and Workforce Development**: Computers are necessary for education and workforce development, according to research. They give people access to online training, education, and skill-development programs so they can gain the information and abilities necessary to work in the digital economy.

1.5.8. **Efficient Communication**: Computers facilitate efficient communication both within and across companies. By bridging geographical boundaries, this better communication fosters collaboration, streamlines procedures, and fosters creativity.

1.5.9. **Improved Customer Experience**: Personalized marketing, e-commerce platforms, and customer relationship management (CRM) systems are a few ways that businesses use computers to improve consumer experiences. Through increasing sales and client retention, this promotes customer loyalty and promotes economic progress.

1.5.10. **Infrastructure Development**: Development of vital infrastructure, such as data centres, telecommunications networks, and high-speed internet access, is frequently a result of investments in computer technology. In the digital age, this infrastructure is essential for economic progress.

Thus, computers have played a significant role in both economic growth and the acceleration of innovation across a range of industries. Their pivotal influence on productivity, connection, and the emergence of new industries highlights their function as engines of economic development in the contemporary era.

1.6. Personal Productivity Empowerment:

Computer systems have made it possible for people to easily organize work, manage schedules, and create content, thanks to word processing software and productivity apps. Workflows have been streamlined by spreadsheets, presentations, and digital collaboration tools, increasing productivity on both a personal and professional level.

The process of applying tools, tactics, and strategies to improve one's efficiency, effectiveness, and overall productivity in a variety of spheres of life, including job, education, and personal activities, is referred to as personal productivity empowerment. The empowering of personal productivity is significantly aided by computers and digital technologies.

They assist in this empowerment in the following ways:

1.6.1. **Task Management and Organization**: To-do list apps, calendar tools, and project management platforms all assist people in effectively organizing their tasks, setting priorities, and managing deadlines. Better time management and productivity are aided by this digital structure.

1.6.2. **Digital Note-Taking**: Is made possible by computers and tablets and can be more streamlined and searchable than traditional paper notes. Users may store, organize, and access their notes from anywhere with the help of apps like Evernote, OneNote, and Notion.

1.6.3. **Time Tracking**: Time tracking software enables users to keep track of their time usage, spot time-wasting habits, and make necessary adjustments to increase productivity. This is particularly helpful for professionals and independent contractors that charge by the hour.

1.6.4. **Email Management**: To help manage email overload, email applications and solutions provide features like filters, folders, and automated responses. They make it possible for people to keep their inboxes clear of junk and respond to critical messages more quickly.

1.6.5. **Collaboration and Communication**: Email, instant messaging, video conferencing, and collaboration platforms like Microsoft Teams and Slack are all made possible by computers. These tools boost productivity by facilitating remote work and increasing teamwork.

1.6.6. **Automation:** Tools and scripts can be programmed to carry out time-consuming and repetitive chores, freeing up people to concentrate on more significant and creative work. For instance, automating report generation or data entry can save a lot of time.

1.6.7. **Digital Learning:** People can learn at their own pace by taking online classes and using e-learning platforms that are available through computers. The continual learning supports both professional and personal development.

1.6.8. **Research and Information Gathering**: Access to information is made simpler by the internet, search engines, and databases. People can use computers to perform research, collect data, and keep up with news and developments in their sector.

1.6.9. **Cloud Storage and File Sharing:** Users can save, read, and share documents and files using cloud storage services like Google Drive and Dropbox from any device with an internet connection. This makes collaboration easier and guarantees data accessibility.

1.6.10. **Personal Finance Management:** Tools for keeping track of spending, developing budgets, and managing investments are available in personal finance software and apps. Better financial decisions and more savings may result from this financial empowerment.

1.6.11. **Health and Wellness Tracking:** Tracking one's physical activity, sleep habits, and diet is made possible through health and fitness applications and wearables, which are frequently connected to computers and smartphones. This supports well-being and better lifestyles.

1.6.12. **Creativity and Content Creation:** Computers with software for graphic design, video editing, writing, and music production enable people to express their creativity and turn concepts into usable objects or works of art.

1.6.13. **Remote Work and Flexibility:** Computers provide remote work and flexible work arrangements, providing people greater choice over their work schedules and environments. This could improve overall job satisfaction and work-life balance.

Thus, personal productivity empowerment via computers and digital technologies enables people to regain control over their personal and professional lives. Better organization, communication, and work automation are made possible by these tools, which eventually improve output, effectiveness, and quality of life.

1.7. Research and Educational Advancements:

The availability of huge informational resources thanks to computer systems has revolutionized both education and research. Online libraries, digital textbooks, and e-learning tools have made knowledge sharing more accessible, promoting academic advancement and facilitating lifelong learning.

Computers and digital technology have had a significant impact on research and educational breakthroughs in a variety of ways. There has been substantial advancement in many sectors as a result of the transformation of research, teaching, and learning processes brought about by the integration of these technologies. Here are a few significant ways that computers have advanced science and education:

1.7.1. Research Developments

a. **Data collecting and Analysis**: The collecting and analysis of data in scientific study has been completely transformed by computers. With the use of sophisticated software, researchers may gather and store enormous volumes of data digitally, analyse it, and display the findings for more thorough and accurate research.
b. **Simulation and Modelling**: High-performance computing allows for the creation of intricate simulations and mathematical models. Computer simulations of experiments are used by researchers in disciplines including physics, climate science, and biology to gain a deeper understanding.
c. **Data sharing and Collaborations:** Digital platforms and technologies make it easier for scholars throughout the

world to share and collaborate on data. By enabling researchers to build upon one another's work and access common databases, this quickens the speed of research.

d. **Genomic Research:** Genetics and tailored medicine both largely rely on genomic sequencing and analysis, which is why improved computational power is so important. Large amounts of genetic data can be processed and interpreted thanks to computers.
e. **AI and Machine Learning:** Artificial intelligence (AI) and machine learning have transformed data analysis, pattern identification, and predictive modelling in a variety of industries, including healthcare, finance, and materials science.
f. **Scientific Visualization:** With the use of computers, researchers may produce elaborate visual representations of scientific data that help make difficult subjects easier to grasp. This makes it easier to communicate findings to the general public and experts.
g. **Remote Sensing and Satellite Technology:** Computers are essential for processing data from satellites and remote sensors in remote sensing and satellite technology. For observing environmental changes, predicting the weather, and managing disasters, this knowledge is essential.
h. **Drug Discovery**: Computers are used in computational chemistry and bioinformatics to screen and simulate prospective drug molecules, greatly speeding up the process of discovering new drugs.

1.7.2. **Educational Progress**:

a. **Online Learning:** Thanks to the development of computers, students of different ages and educational backgrounds now have access to a wide variety of courses and materials. Education has become more accessible and democratic as a result.

b. **Interactive Learning:** Learning that is interactive and engaging is enhanced by educational software and simulations. Through computer programs, students can investigate complicated ideas, deepening their comprehension of disciplines like science and arithmetic.

c. **Personalised Learning**: Computers may modify educational material to suit the requirements and development of specific pupils, providing individualized learning experiences. This enables pupils to work through their individual learning problems and learn at their own speed.

d. **Digital Libraries and Resources**: Students and researchers can more easily access material and conduct literature reviews thanks to computers' access to sizable digital libraries, scholarly journals, and research databases.

e. **Collaborative Learning:** Online collaboration tools and platforms help students and teachers work together on group projects and discussions, which promotes collaborative learning.

f. **Inclusivity and Accessibility**: Computers have made it easier for people with disabilities to use them. People with impairments can now access educational resources and take part in online education thanks to assistive technologies and software.

g. **Support for Teachers:** Computers help teachers with lesson planning, grading, and classroom administration. Administrative tasks are streamlined by learning management systems (LMS), allowing teachers to concentrate more on instruction.

h. **Global Learning:** Online exchange programs and video

conferencing bring together students and teachers from all over the world, fostering intercultural communication and global cooperation.

Thus, computers have significantly contributed to the advancement of research and education by offering tools for data analysis, simulation, teamwork, and access to a great amount of resources. They have democratized education, hastened the advancement of research, and created new opportunities for learning and discovery across a variety of disciplines.

1.8. Scientific and Medical Breakthroughs

Computer systems are essential for data analysis, simulations, and difficult computations in both healthcare and science. They assist in the modelling of complex biological processes, drug discovery, genetic analysis, and medical imaging. Scientific and medical advancements have been greatly aided by computers and other digital technologies. They have significantly advanced these sectors by revolutionizing research, data analysis, and the provision of healthcare services. Here are a few ways that computers have aided in the advancement of science and medicine:

1.8.1. Scientific Innovations

a. **Data Analysis:** Thanks to computers, scientists can now handle and examine huge datasets that were produced as a result of experiments and observations. Breakthroughs in disciplines including genetics, particle physics, and climate science have resulted from this.
b. **Simulating and Modelling:** Complex systems and processes is made possible by high-performance computing. Understanding everything from molecular interactions to the behaviour of galaxies has benefited from this.
c. **Drug Discovery:** The development of new drugs has been sped up by computational techniques and algorithms running on powerful computers. Molecular dynamics simulations and virtual compound screening make the process of finding prospective medication candidates more effective.
d. **Scientific Visualisation:** Computers are used in scientific visualization to produce visual representations of scientific

data. This helps with scientific communication and understanding by facilitating the understanding of complicated concepts by researchers and the general public.

e. **AI and Machine Learning:** Patterns and insights in data that were previously challenging or impossible to find are now being found using machine learning and artificial intelligence. Applications of these technologies can be found in astronomy, biology, and chemistry.
f. **Genomic Research:** Significant strides in genomics have been made thanks to developments in DNA sequencing and computational biology. Now that complete genomes can be quickly analysed, genetics and tailored therapy are being improved.

1.8.2. Medical Breakthroughs

a. **Medical Imaging:** Computers are necessary for medical imaging procedures including X-rays, CT scans, and MRIs. Using cutting-edge image processing and analysis techniques, diseases and ailments can be accurately diagnosed.
b. **Drug Development:** Computers are essential to the design and development of pharmaceuticals. The drug development process is accelerated by the use of computational chemistry and virtual screening to find prospective drug candidates.
c. **Genomic Medicine:** High-performance computer has enabled genomic sequencing and analysis, which has resulted in individualized medicine. A significant advance in healthcare is the ability to customize a patient's course of therapy depending on their genetic composition.
d. **Telemedicine:** Through the use of computers and other digital technology, healthcare services are now more

accessible. Remote consultations between patients and medical professionals increase access to care.

e. **Electronic Health Records (EHRs):** EHR systems digitally store patient medical records, facilitating access to and sharing of patient data by healthcare providers. This improves the coordination of patient care and lowers mistakes.
f. **Medical Research and Clinical Trials**: Computers are used in medical research and clinical trials to manage and analyse the data, which enables researchers to assess the efficacy and safety of novel therapies and treatments.
g. **Modelling and Forecasting Diseases**: Computer models are used to mimic the transmission of diseases and forecast outbreaks. Understanding how the virus behaves and using that information to direct public health initiatives have been essential throughout the COVID-19 pandemic.
h. **Robotics Assisted Surgery:** Computer-controlled robotic equipment help surgeons carry out minimally invasive treatments with higher precision, minimizing patient trauma and speeding up recovery.
i. **AI in Healthcare:** Machine learning and artificial intelligence are being used to evaluate medical data, help with diagnosis, and forecast patient outcomes. AI has showed promise in spotting patterns in medical photos and detecting early signs of cancer.

Thus, the use of computers and digital technology has greatly advanced both science and medicine. They have improved modelling, visualization, and data processing, which has sparked ground-breaking research in many different sectors of science. These technological advancements have ushered in a new era of customized medicine and innovation in medicine by enhancing diagnosis, treatment, and patient care.

1.9. Entertainment and Creative Expression:

The entertainment sector, from video games and streaming services to digital art and music production, depends heavily on computers. The definition of creativity and artistic expression has been altered by computer graphics, animation, and virtual reality. Computer systems are used in environmental monitoring and conservation activities.

Computers and digital technologies have significantly changed entertainment and creative expression. New opportunities for artistic production, dissemination, and consumption across numerous media and entertainment formats have been made possible by these technologies. The following are a few examples of how computers have impacted entertainment and artistic expression:

1.9.1. Creating Movies And Videos:

- **Digital Film Making**: Computers have transformed the movie business by making digital filmmaking possible. The use of digital cameras, editing programs, and visual effects equipment has made it simpler and more affordable to create high-quality movies and videos.
- **Visual Effects (VFX):** Thanks to computers, complex visual effects and CGI (Computer-Generated Imagery) are now feasible, enabling blockbuster films to feature breath-taking and lifelike effects.
- **Animation:** To produce visually appealing films, animation studios employ computer animation tools to produce both 2D and 3D animations.

1.9.2. Music Creation and Production:

- **Digital Audio Works (DAW):** Musicians and producers utilize digital audio workstations (DAWs) to compose, record, edit, and mix music. As a result, music creation has become more accessible, enabling artists to produce high-calibre music in their homes.
- **Electronic Music:** Digital instruments and software play a major part in the creation of electronic music genres like techno, EDM (Electronic Dance Music), and hip-hop, which were made possible by computers.
- **Music Streaming:** To make music recommendations to customers based on their listening preferences, online music streaming services like Spotify and Apple Music use computer algorithms.

1. **Visual And Graphic Arts:**

- **Graphic Design:** To produce digital artwork, logos, and commercials, graphic designers utilize programs like Adobe Photoshop and Illustrator.
- **Digital Illustration:** By allowing artists to create intricate and detailed artwork digitally, digital illustration software and tablets extend the potential for visual expression.

1. **Interactive Entertainment And Gaming**

- **Video Games:** The creation of video games relies heavily on computers, which enable game developers to produce immersive and graphically attractive gaming experiences. High-quality graphics and lifelike simulations are available on gaming consoles and PCs.
- **Virtual Reality (VR) And Augmented Reality (AR):** are computer-driven technologies that offer interactive, immersive gaming experiences as well as uses in training and education.

1. **Writing And Literature:**

- **Digital Publishing**: E-books and other digital publishing tools have revolutionized the book industry. Digital self-publishing allows authors to reach a large audience without the help of established publishing houses.
- **Word Processing:** Writing and word processing software facilitates the drafting and editing of manuscripts by authors. Tools for formatting, grammar checking, and spell-checking make writing easier.

1. **Television and Streaming Services:**

- **Streaming Content:** To provide users with tailored content recommendations, online streaming services like Netflix, Amazon Prime Video, and Hulu employ algorithms and computer systems.
- **Content Creation:** YouTube and other platforms for user-generated content provide people the power to make, distribute, and earn money from their videos and other works, democratizing the entertainment sector.

1. **Social Media and Digital Art:**

- **Digital Art:** Using software and digital technologies, digital artists produce beautiful works of art that they then post to internet galleries and social media sites.
- **User-Generated Content:** Social media platforms give users the opportunity to share their original works of art, music, writing, and video with a large audience.
- **Live Streaming:** On websites like Twitch and YouTube Live, content producers may share their work in real time with viewers.

Thus, the democratization of the creative process and the expansion of opportunities for artists and entertainers to connect with a global audience have been two major impacts of computers and digital technology on entertainment and creative expression. Additionally, they have improved the level of engagement and quality of entertainment experiences, making it simpler for individuals to interact with different media and express themselves.

1.10. Environmental Monitoring and Sustainability:

To support sustainability, they aid in monitoring climate patterns, forecasting natural calamities, and managing renewable energy sources. Efforts to monitor the environment and promote sustainability have greatly benefited from computers and digital technologies. With the aid of these technologies, academics, governments, and organizations may monitor the environment, make informed decisions, and work toward a more sustainable future. These technologies also provide tools for data collecting, analysis, and communication. Here are a few ways that computers support sustainability and environmental monitoring:

1.10.1. Environmental Surveillance

- **Remote Sensing**: Is the process of gathering information about the Earth's surface, atmosphere, and oceans using computerized satellites. Monitoring environmental changes, such as deforestation, urbanization, and climatic patterns, requires the use of this information.

- **Weather Forecasting:** Complex weather models that forecast weather patterns, natural disasters, and extreme events are run on supercomputers. Disaster preparedness and reaction are aided by these projections.
- **Air Quality Monitoring:** Computerized sensors and networks monitor the air quality in metropolitan areas to assist pinpoint the sources of pollution and determine how it may affect people's health. The general public is frequently given access to real-time data.
- **Water Quality Assessment**: Automated sensors and

computer systems keep track of the water quality in rivers, lakes, and seas. This information is useful for locating sources of pollution, managing water resources, and preserving aquatic habitats.

- **Wildlife Tracking**: Researchers can follow and examine the movements and activities of wildlife populations by using computers to process data from GPS trackers, satellite tags, and video traps.
- **Environmental Data Management**: Computers make it easier for scientists and decision-makers to access and use huge volumes of environmental data by facilitating their storage, management, and analysis.

1.10.2. Initiatives for Sustainability:

- **Energy Management:** Smart grids and automated energy management systems aid in the efficient distribution of energy, the reduction of energy waste, and the integration of renewable energy sources into the grid.
- **Smart Buildings:** To enhance energy efficiency in both commercial and residential structures, computerized building management systems regulate lighting, heating, and cooling. The use of automated controls and occupancy sensors can help save energy.
- **Transport Efficiency:** Transport network optimization, traffic congestion reduction, and the promotion of environmentally friendly transportation methods like carpooling and public transportation are all achieved through the use of computer algorithms and traffic management systems.
- **Waste Management**: Computerized waste management systems keep tabs on and improve rubbish collection routes, cutting down on fuel use and greenhouse gas emissions. Gas

emissions and landfill conditions can both be tracked via sensors.

- **Precision Agriculture:** GPS-guided tractors, drones, and sensors, as well as other precision agriculture techniques that increase crop yields, consume less resources, and have less of an impact on the environment, are made possible by computers and digital technologies.
- **Environmentally Friendly Manufacturing:** Systems for computer-aided design (CAD) and computer-aided manufacturing (CAM) assist create products and procedures that use the least amount of energy and materials possible.

1.10.3. Conservation Restoration:

- **Environmental Modelling:** Scientists and conservationists use computers to build models that imitate ecosystems to better understand how climate change and human activity affect biodiversity.
- **Reforestation and Habitat Restoration**: Geographic Information Systems (GIS) and digital mapping tools help locate places for reforestation and habitat restoration, maximizing conservation efforts.
- **Eco-friendly Technologies:** The development of eco-friendly technologies, such as enhanced water purification techniques, energy-efficient appliances, and sustainable building materials, is aided by computational simulations and materials science.
- **Ocean Conservation:** To investigate, monitor, and track endangered species, autonomous underwater vehicles (AUVs) are outfitted with computer systems.

In summary, computers and digital technology are essential for improving conservation efforts, supporting sustainability projects, and monitoring the environment. In addition to encouraging sustainable habits and technology, they offer the data processing power, modelling capabilities, and communication tools required for comprehending and addressing environmental concerns.

1.11. Social Impact and Connectivity:

By increasing public knowledge of social issues and facilitating grassroots movements, computer systems have sparked social change. They create forums for lobbying, activism, and community development as well as enable the exchange of various viewpoints. Computers and other digital technology have significantly changed how people interact, communicate, and connect in society. They have changed how people interact with one another, made the world more connected, and had an impact on many other facets of human conduct. The following are a few significant ways that computers and digital technologies have impacted society and connectivity:

1.11.1 Social Interaction and Communication:

- **Social Media:** Websites like Facebook, Twitter, Instagram, and LinkedIn make it possible for users to interact with one another, share experiences, and speak with friends, family, and co-workers anywhere in the globe. Modern social interaction has mostly moved online thanks to social media.
- **Instant Messaging**: By enabling real-time communication through messaging apps like WhatsApp, Messenger, and WeChat, people can keep in touch and send and receive messages, photographs, and videos right away.
- **Online Communities**: Internet forums, discussion boards, and social networking sites help people with similar interests and ideas communicate with each other and form online communities.
- **Video Calls:** Video calling is supported by computers and cell-phones, enabling people to speak face-to-face with loved ones even when they are thousands of miles apart.

1.11.2 Worldwide Connections:

- **Internet Access:** Computers have made it possible for people from all walks of life to connect to the internet and a wealth of online information.
- **E-commerce:** Online marketplaces and e-commerce platforms have made it possible for businesses to expand internationally and for consumers to buy things from all over the world.
- **Remote Work and Education**: Computers support online learning and remote work, removing geographical restrictions and allowing people to work or study from any location with an internet connection.

1.11.3 Sharing and Awareness of Information:

- **News and Information**: Real-time updates and a variety of viewpoints on current events are provided via digital news sources, blogs, and social media, enhancing information availability and awareness.
- **Citizen Journalism:** Computers give people the ability to report on and share news and events, which supports citizen journalism and grassroots movements.

1.11.4 Social Advocacy and Activism:

- **Online Petitions and Campaigns:** Can be created and promoted thanks to digital platforms, which make it simpler for people and organizations to support social and environmental causes.
- **Awareness and Education**: Computers help spread awareness and educate people about social concerns by way of online movies, educational websites, and social media

initiatives.

1.11.5. Exchange of Cultures and Creativity

- **Digital Art and Expression**: Computers offer tools for artistic expression, allowing musicians, writers, and content producers to share their work online and reach a global audience.
- **Cultural Exchange**: Through websites like YouTube, where people can share insights into their cultures, traditions, and languages, computers encourage cross-cultural exchange.

1. **Problems And Worries:**

- **Digital Divide:** Despite the benefits of connectivity that computers and digital technologies provide, there is still a digital divide since some communities lack access to dependable internet and technology, which exacerbates social inequities.
- **Privacy and Security:** As people and companies share personal information and carry out transactions online, worries about online privacy and data security have emerged.
- **Online Harassment:** Because of the anonymity of the internet, problems like cyberbullying and online harassment have emerged, raising questions about people's psychological health.
- **Filter Bubbles:** Social media platforms' and search engines' algorithms can produce "filter bubbles," in which people are only exposed to material and opinions that support their own ideas, potentially limiting their exposure to other points of view.

In conclusion, computers and digital technologies have had a big impact on society because they have made it easier for people to communicate, connect to the world, share information, and trade cultures. Despite the many advantages they have provided, they have also sparked worries about privacy, online conduct, and access disparities. A continuing societal concern is finding a balance between the benefits to society and the difficulties.

1.12. Automation and the Transformation of Industries:

From manufacturing to logistics, automation is driven by computer systems. Artificial intelligence, machine learning, and robotics improve productivity, lessen human error, and enable the development of new goods and services.

Computers and digital technology have profoundly changed sectors thanks to automation, which also changed the nature of employment and enhanced productivity.

Here are a few significant effects of automation on various industries:

1.12.1. Production and Manufacturing

- **Industrial Robotics**: Computer-controlled robots carry out a variety of production duties, such as product assembly and quality inspection. Higher accuracy, more output, and lower labour costs are the results of this.
- **CNC (Computer Numerical Control) Machining:** CNC machines precisely control machining tools using computer programming, resulting in highly accurate and efficient manufacturing processes.
- **3D Printing:** Additive manufacturing techniques powered by computers enable quick product prototype and customization, upending conventional production processes.

1. **Transport and Logistics:**

- **Automated Warehousing**: Warehousing and distribution centres are automated thanks to computers and robotics, which eliminates the need for manual labour for jobs like order picking and packaging.

- **Autonomous Vehicles:** Could revolutionize the logistics and transportation sectors. Self-driving cars and trucks use computers and sensors to manoeuver and move cargo.

1. **Banking and Finance:**

- **Algorithmic Trading**: Since computers can carry out intricate financial transactions quickly, algorithmic trading has become a major player in the financial markets.
- **Online Banking and Payments**: Automated financial transactions are made possible by digital banking and online payment systems, which eliminates the need for physical branches and currency.

1. **Healthcare:**

- **Medical Imaging:** Computer-aided diagnosis (CAD) technologies help radiologists interpret medical images, enhancing accuracy and productivity in healthcare.
- **Robotic Surgery**: Computers direct surgical robots that let surgeons carry out minimally invasive procedures.

1. **Customer Support and Service:**

- **Chatbots and Virtual Assistants:** Automated chatbots and virtual assistants manage customer assistance and questions, giving prompt answers and obviating the need for human operators.
- **Automated Call-Centres**: Interactive voice response (IVR) systems use digital menus to route and manage incoming calls, optimizing customer support operations.

1. **Agriculture:**

- **Precision Agriculture:** By optimizing the planting, fertilizing, and harvesting processes, computers and GPS technology enable precision agriculture, which increases crop yields and uses less resources.

1.12.7. Retail and online shopping:

- **Automated Checkout:** The necessity for human cashiers in retail outlets is reduced by self-checkout kiosks and automated cashier-less stores.
- **Systems for Product Recommendations**: Online merchants utilize algorithms to examine consumer preferences and make tailored product recommendations that increase sales.

1. **Utility and Energy:**

- **Smart Grids:** Computerized "smart grids" optimize energy distribution, lower power interruptions, and facilitate the incorporation of renewable energy sources.

1. **Building And Architecture**

- **Building Information Modelling (BIM):** BIM software and computers help architects and engineers plan and design construction projects more effectively, resulting in fewer mistakes and reworks.
- **Construction Automation:** Robots and automated equipment are being utilized more frequently in the construction industry to do activities like bricklaying, pouring concrete, and demolition.

1. **Training and Education**

- **E-learning Platforms:** The automation of the delivery of educational content has been made possible by computers and digital technology, enabling online courses and individualized learning experiences.
- **Simulated Training:** To provide realistic training for professionals in fields like aviation and healthcare, virtual simulations and computer-driven training programs are

used.

While automation has many advantages, such as improved productivity and decreased human error, it has also prompted questions about job loss, the need to retrain the workforce, and moral issues around the employment of AI and robotics. For businesses and regulators, finding a balance between technology and human work is a constant issue.

In essence, computer systems have shaped how humans connect, learn, work, and invent in modern civilization. Beyond technology, they play an important role in advancing socioeconomic progress, cross-cultural dialogue, and connection on a global scale. Computer systems will continue to stimulate advancement, amplify human potential, and redefine the possibilities of what may be accomplished in the digital age as technology develops.

Chapter 2: Hardware Components

2.1. Central Processing Unit (CPU)

The most significant processor in a computer is termed a central processing unit (CPU), sometimes known as a central processor or main processor. Its electronic circuitry carries out a computer program's instructions, carrying out functions like input/output (I/O), logic, and controlling. This function contrasts with that of specialist coprocessors like graphics processing units (GPUs) and external components like main memory and I/O hardware.

Although CPUs' shape, design, and implementation have evolved throughout time, their basic function has remained mostly same. The arithmetic-logic unit (ALU), which performs arithmetic and logic operations, processor registers, which provide operands to the ALU and store the results of ALU operations, and a control unit, which coordinates the fetching (from memory), decoding, and execution (of instructions), are the main components of a CPU.

With one or more CPUs on a single IC chip, integrated circuit (IC) microprocessors are how most current CPUs are implemented. Multi-core processors are microprocessor chips with multiple CPUs. Additionally, multiple virtual or logical CPUs can be created by multitasking the separate physical CPUs, or processor cores. Such integrated devices, also known as microcontrollers or systems on a chip (SoC), can include a CPU, memory, peripheral ports, and other computer components. Multiple processors work simultaneously in array or vector processors, and no component is regarded as the central processing unit. Virtual CPUs are an abstraction of computational resources that are dynamically aggregated.

2.2. Memory Hierarchy: RAM, Cache, and Storage

The memory hierarchy in computer organization divides computer storage into a hierarchy based on reaction time. Due to the relationships between reaction time, complexity, and capacity, the levels can also be separated based on their performance and regulating methods. Performance in algorithm predictions, lower level programming constructs requiring locality of reference, and computer architectural design are all impacted by memory hierarchy.

The size and capabilities of each component must be taken into account while designing for high performance in order to work within the constraints of the memory hierarchy. Each of the different components can be thought of as a member of a hierarchy of memory (m1, m2,.......mn), each of which is smaller and faster than the mi+1 member above it in the hierarchy. A lower level will react by filling a buffer and then signalling for the transfer to be activated in order to reduce waiting by upper levels.

There are four main levels of storage.

- **Internal:** Processor registers and cache are internal.
- **Main:** The system RAM and controller cards make up the main.
- **Online Mass Storage**: Secondary storage using online mass storage.
- **Offline Bulk Storage**: Tertiary and off-line storage for bulk data off-line.

This is a basic hierarchy of memory organizing. There are many other useful structures. When developing a computer architecture, one may, for instance, take the paging algorithm into account as a level for virtual memory and include a level of near line storage between online and offline storage.

2.2.1. Why Does the System Need Memory Hierarchy?

One of the most essential components of computer memory is the memory hierarchy, which aids in the computer's memory optimization. The memory is divided into several levels, each of which varies in size, price, etc. Cache and main memory, for example, are faster than other types of memory but have a little less space and are more expensive, whereas other memory has a little higher storage value but is a little slower. There are several types of memory, and different types of memory have different access speeds for data.

2.2.1.1. Memory Hierarchy Designs

2.2.1.1.1. **Registers:** Registers are compact, high-speed memory components found inside the CPU. The most commonly utilized information and instructions are kept in them. The quickest access time and smallest storage capacity are found in registers, which typically range from 16 to 64 bits.

2.2.1.1.2. **Cache Memory:** A compact, quick memory device called cache memory is placed near to the CPU. It keeps track of commonly used information and commands that have recently been accessed from the main memory. By giving the CPU quick access to commonly used data, cache memory helps reduce the amount of time it takes to access data.

2.2.1.1.3. **Main Memory:** The main memory of a computer system is also referred to as RAM (*Random Access Memory*). Although it is slower than cache memory, it has more storage space. Data and instructions that are currently being used by the CPU are kept in main memory.

2.2.1.2. Main Memory Types

2.2.1.2.1. Static RAM: Static RAM uses flip-flops to store binary data, and the data is valid as long as power is applied. It is utilized to implement cache memory because of its quicker access time.

2.2.1.2.2. Dynamic RAM: It stores binary data on a capacitor as a charge. After a few milliseconds, it requires renewing circuitry to keep the capacitors charged. Compared to, it has more memory cells per unit of space.

2.2.1.2.3. Secondary Storage: Secondary storage is a non-volatile memory component that has a greater storage capacity than primary memory, such as hard disk drives (HDD) and solid-state drives (SSD). It is used to store information and instructions that the CPU is not currently using. In the memory hierarchy, secondary storage has the slowest access speed and is often the cheapest type of memory.

2.2.1.2.4. Magnetized Disk: Simply put, magnetic disks are circular plates that can be made out of magnetized materials, magnetized metal, or plastic. The computer's magnetic disks, which are commonly used, operate at a rapid speed.

2.2.1.2.5. Magnetized Tape: Simply put, magnetic tape is a magnetic recording device that has a plastic layer on top of it. It is typically employed for data backup. Because a computer's access time for a magnetic tape is a little slower, accessing the strip from the tape takes some time.

2.2.1.3. Features of the Memory Hierarchy

2.2.1.3.1. Capacity: This refers to the total amount of data that the memory can hold. The capacity rises from the top to the bottom of the Hierarchy.

2.2.1.3.2. Access Time: This is the amount of time that passes between a read-write request and the data becoming available. The access time increases from top to bottom of the Hierarchy.

2.2.1.3.3. Performance: Previously, when the computer system wasn't created with a Memory Hierarchy design, the speed gap between the CPU registers and Main Memory grew as a result of a significant difference in access time. The system's performance suffers as a result, necessitating improvement. Memory Hierarchy Design was used to make this improvement, which has increased system performance. Reduced memory hierarchy depth required for data manipulation is one of the most important techniques to improve system performance.

2.2.1.3.4. Cost per Bit: The cost per bit rises from bottom to top in the hierarchy, therefore internal memory is more expensive than external memory.

2.2.1.4. Advantages of Memory Hierarchy

- It aids in dispersing data around the computer network.
- It assists in lessening some degradation and improving memory management.

- It helps consumers save money and time.

2.3. Input and Output Devices

Any hardware that enables a human operator or other systems to interface with a computer is referred to as an input/output (IO) device. As the name suggests, input/output devices have the ability to both input and output data to and from a computer. A piece of hardware that can take, output, or process data is known as an input/output (I/O) device. It receives data as input, gives it to a computer as a computer output, and also transfers computer data to storage media.

2.3.1. Input Devices

The devices that are used to provide signals to the computer so it can accomplish tasks are known as input devices. The Central Processing Unit, or CPU, is the receiver at the other end and is responsible for sending signals to the output devices.

The following are some categories for input devices:

- Keyboard
- Pointing Tools
- Composite Technology
- Gaming Console
- Visual Equipment
- Devices for Audio Input

The following describes a few of the input devices.

2.3.1.1. **Keyboard:** The most frequent and popular input method for entering data onto a computer is the keyboard. The keyboard layout resembles a standard typewriter even if there are several extra keys for conducting various functions. Although there are already keyboards with 104 keys or 108 keys available for Windows and the Internet, keyboards typically come in two sizes: 84 keys or 101/102 keys.

2.3.1.2. **Mouse:** The mouse is the most used pointing device. A small cursor is moved across the screen by clicking and dragging the mouse. When you release the mouse, the cursor will cease moving. The mouse must be moved by you in order for the computer to move; it cannot move by itself. It serves as an input device as a result. A mouse is an input device that enables you to control the position and movement of the on-screen cursor/pointer by moving the mouse on a flat surface. When the right mouse button is clicked, more options are displayed, while the left mouse button can be used to select or move objects.

2.3.1.3. **Track Ball:** The Track Ball is a laptop and notebook attachment that replaces the function of a mouse. Its structure is comparable to that of a mouse. Its construction resembles a half-inserted ball, and moving the cursor is done using the fingers. For this, various shapes such as balls, buttons, and squares are employed.

2.3.1.4. **Joystick:** On a computer screen, a joystick is a pointing tool used to move the pointer. Each of the stick's bottom and top ends is fitted with a spherical ball. The lower spherical ball slips in a socket. The joystick can be moved in all four directions. The joystick performs similar duties to a mouse. Computer video games and CAD (Computer-Aided Design) are the two main uses for it.

2.3.1.5. **Bar Code Readers:** Using bright and dark lines to represent the data, a bar code reader is a device that reads bar-coded information. Bar-coded information is frequently used to label items, number books, and other things. It might be a component of a stationary scanner or a handheld scanner. Using a bar code reader, a bar code image is scanned, converted to an alphanumeric value, and sent to the computer.

2.3.1.6. **Little Pen:** A pointing tool that resembles a pen is called a light pen. It can be used to the monitor screen to draw or to choose a menu item. A tiny tube contains an optical system and a photocell. When the pen button is pressed and the tip of a light pen is moved across a monitor screen, the photocell sensor element recognizes the screen location and sends a signal.

2.3.1.7. **Scanner:** Scanners are input devices with similar capabilities as photocopiers. When information on paper needs to be moved to the computer's hard drive for further modification, this technique is used. The raw photos are gathered by the scanner, which then transforms them into a digital format that can be saved on a disc. These images can be changed before printing.

2.3.1.8. **OCR, Or Optical Character Recognition:** A machine called an OCR, or optical character recognition, reads printed text. OCR optically scans the text and reads each character individually.

2.3.1.9. **OMR, Or Optical Mark Reader:** A tool called an optical mark reader is typically employed in educational institutions to verify the responses to objective exams. It is capable of identifying pencil and pen marks.

2.3.1.10. **Magnetic Ink Character Recognition (MICR):** It is a tool that is typically utilized in banks to manage the customer-given checks. It facilitates deciphering the magnetic ink on the code number and check number. Compared to other processes, this one is very quick.

2.3.1.11. **Web Camera:** A webcam is an input device since it captures a video image of the scene in front of it. It is either integrated into the computer (such as a laptop) or connected via a USB port. A webcam is a tiny digital video camera that is connected to a computer. Since it can both take pictures and record videos, it is also referred to as a web camera. To stream video in real-time over the Internet, these cameras come with software that needs to be installed on the computer. It can record HD films and photographs, although the video quality isn't as excellent as that of other cameras (in mobiles, other gadgets, or regular cameras).

2.3.1.12. **Digitizer:** The process of converting analog signals to digital signals is known as digitization. It transforms signals into numbers. A graphic tablet, which is used to transform graphics into binary data, is an illustration of a digitizer.

2.3.1.13. **Microphone:** The microphone performs the function of an input device by taking in voice signals and translating them to digital format. Every device that has anything to do with music has this very ubiquitous device.

2.3.2. Output Devices

The devices known as output devices are those that display the outcome of our input to a computer system. The output can take on a variety of various forms, including visual, aural, and visual.

The list of output devices and descriptions follows.

2.3.2.1. **Visual Display Units (VDUs):** Commonly referred to as monitors, are a computer's main means of output. It arranges tiny dots, referred to as pixels, in a rectangular arrangement to produce images. The sharpness of the image depends on the number of pixels.

Below is a description of the two types of monitor viewing screens.

Cathode-Ray Tube (CRT) Monitor: A CRT display is made up of microscopic pixels. The pixels become smaller as the image quality or resolution increases.

Flat-Panel Monitor: A flat-panel display is a style of video display that uses less volume, weight, and power than a CRT. They can be worn on the wrist or hung from the wall. Currently, laptop computers, monitors, video games, calculators, and graphical user interfaces all employ flat-panel displays.

2.3.2.2. **Television:** One of the common output devices found in every home is the television. As the user operates the television, video and audio files are displayed on the screen. As opposed to CRT screens that we previously utilized, plasma displays are what we use today.

2.3.2.3. **Printers**: Printer Information can be printed on paper using printers, which are output devices. The following describes many types of printers:

- Character printers with an impact
- Line Printers
- Impact-Free Printers
- Inkjet printers
- Laser Printers
- Inkjet Printer

1. **Impact Printer:** In impact printers, characters are imprinted on the ribbon before it is crumpled up against the paper. Impact printers have the qualities listed below:

- Very Noisy
- Exceptionally low cost per consumable.
- Only one character can be printed at a time with the Character Printer. There are two kinds.
- Large-scale printing works best with it because of how inexpensive it is.
- There is direct physical contact with the paper to produce a picture.

1. **Line Printers:** Line Printers are printers with the ability to print one line at a time.

- Chain Printer
- Drum Printer

1. **Impact-Free Printers:** In non-impact printers, characters can be produced without the use of a ribbon. These printers are also referred to as Page Printers because they print an entire page at once. The properties of non-impact printers are as

follows:

- Superior quality
- Faster
- They don't create much noise.
- Range of fonts and character sizes supported

1. **Character Printers:** There are two kinds.

- Daisy Wheel
- Dot Matrix Printer

1. **Inkjet printers:** Spray technology is used by inkjet printers to print on paper. An inkjet printer can generate papers of a high calibre. Additionally, they print in colour.
2. **Laser Printers:** Laser printers create characters on the page by using dots created by laser lights.
3. **Projector:** Projectors are optical devices that are used to display images on both stationary and moving screens. It aids in visual display on a large screen. Typically, projectors are utilized in theatres, auditoriums, etc.
4. **Speakers:** Are machines that produce sound in response to a computer's command. Speakers today feature wireless technology, like Bluetooth speakers.
5. **Plotter:** A plotter is a tool that assists in creating graphics or other visuals that provide a realistic perspective. To utilize these devices, a graphic card is a need. These pen-like tools aid in producing precise patterns on the computer.
6. **Reader for Braille:** Blind users use Braille Readers, which are crucial tools. Running their fingertips over the device allows those with poor

vision or no vision to easily grasp the data. It is a crucial tool for blind people since it makes it comfortable for them to comprehend letters, alphabets, and other symbols, which aids in their academic pursuits.

7. **Video Card:** A device that is inserted into the computer's motherboard is called a video card. It facilitates the creation of digital content on output devices. It is a valuable tool that enables people to use several different gadgets.
8. **GPS, or Global Positioning System:** The user of the Global Positioning System can get directions thanks to the system, which tracks users' geographical locations using satellite technology. GPS generates precise findings through constant latitudinal and longitudinal calculations. These days, GPS is incorporated into every smart gadget.
9. **Headphones:** Similar to speakers, which are typically used by a single person and are not frequently utilized in big spaces, headphones are a one-person usable item. These are also known as reduced sound frequency headsets.

1. Both The Computer's Input and Output Devices

There are a ton of devices out there that have input and output features. They are capable of carrying out both tasks since they receive data and deliver output.

Following are a few of them.

2.3.3.1. **USB Drive:** A USB drive is one of the devices that can execute input and output operations since it can transfer data from one device to another and back again.

2.3.3.2. **DVD and CD:** The most popular device for preserving data from one computer in a specific format and sending data to other devices that function as input devices for computers is a CD or DVD.

2.3.3.3. **Facsimile:** Fax machines with a scanner and printer that also serve as input and output devices collectively are known as facsimiles.

2.3.3.4. **Modem:** One of the crucial tools for telephonic line-based data transmission is the modem.

2.3.3.5. **Headset:** A speaker and microphone make up the headset; the speaker serves as an output device and the microphone as an input device.

2.4. Motherboard and Expansion Cards

2.4.1. What is a Motherboard?

A computer's motherboard serves as its structural support and links all of its components. Although it has a lot of parts, they are all common and can be found in almost all computers. Usually, more specialized components are not directly mounted on the motherboard, especially those with high costs and/or excessive thermal output. For these parts, a set of sockets is offered instead. There are actually a number of benefits to this design. The end user's choice is the major benefit. Imagine that the RAM, CPU, and GPU were all integrated onto the motherboard. There would need to be numerous motherboards produced by each manufacturer in that scenario.

Users can choose and combine the component combinations they desire or can afford by having these components as separate entities. Future updates are also possible because the components are simple to replace out. The complexity of the motherboards can be reduced by using generic motherboards that allow for the addition of a variety of elements, which keeps costs low and inventory levels high.

Having connectors available also allows for the usage of *daughterboards* that protrude deeper into the open atmosphere. Some components, like RAM and GPUs, are kept cooler as a result. Although coolers might protrude straight from the motherboard, the lack of a clean airflow would reduce cooling effectiveness and become an increasingly serious problem with newer components as power demand rises. Technically, some of the motherboard's sockets aren't thought of as expansion slots. These often serve only one function, like the CPU socket, RAM sockets, and M.2 slots.

However, expansion slots are the more common name for general-purpose slots.

2.4.2. What Is a Slot for Expansion?

Any motherboard slot that may accommodate an expansion card to increase the computer's capability, such as a video card, network card, or sound card, is referred to as an *expansion slot.*

2.4.3. What Purposes Do Expansion Slots Serve?

To give the motherboard easy access to the hardware, the expansion card is inserted straight into the expansion port. It's crucial to open your computer and see what's available before you buy one, though, as there are only so many expansion slots available on each machine.

However, newer computers not only typically have enough expansion slot options but also have functions integrated directly into the motherboard, removing the need for riser boards in some older systems.

2.4.4. Expansion Slots: Historical

Physical expansion slots and the transmission buses they utilize to communicate have historically come in a wide variety. But with contemporary systems, PCIe, a single connector and bus, has prevailed and is used almost exclusively.

Accelerated Graphics Port, or AGP, was a graphics card expansion port in the late 1990s and early 2000s. Because it provided a direct link to system RAM, textures could be stored there instead than in VRAM. It is no longer in use and is absent from motherboards made today. Another expansion port for video cards was the VESA connector. This one, however, was mostly dependent on the Intel 486 CPU and was replaced when Pentium CPUs were introduced.

The AMR expansion slot was used for modem and/or audio cards. In 1998, the Audio Modem Riser was created to support either one or both functionalities. But it was never widely adopted. The Communications and Network Riser, or CNR, was created in 2000 as an update to the AMR standard. It had connectivity for USB, LAN, audio, and modem. A rival standard called the Advanced Communications Riser, or ACR, maintained AMR's backward compatibility. Since the motherboard now houses all functionality, none of these technologies are still in use.

The IBM PC's first expansion slot, known as ISA or Industry Standard Architecture, debuted in 1984. The name is actually a retronym, though. IBM made an attempt to replace it in 1987 using the specialized Micro Channel Architecture, or MCA. As a retaliation, other computer makers worked to establish the Extended Industry Standard Architecture. Neither, though, became popular. Though ISA coexisted with PCI for a while before eventually being dropped from all except legacy devices, both were eventually supplanted by PCI.

2.4.5. Expansion Slots: Current Situation

The expansion slot known as PCI, or Peripheral Component Interconnect, was established in 1992. It was a multipurpose device that was also comparatively fast for the time. Additionally, it featured plug and play, which meant that no adjustments from the user were required for the connected devices to function. In order to provide faster connectivity, PCI-X, with the X standing for "eXtended," was standardized in the server industry in 1998. However, the consumer market didn't really use this much.

When PCIe, also known as PCI Express, was released in 2002, it replaced PCI and PCI-X. Depending on the needed overall bandwidth, PCIe enabled high-speed full duplex transmission with a customizable number of lanes. PCIe swiftly took over as the preferred expansion slot. When the components they served were either integrated into the motherboard or the devices started producing PCIe equivalents, it finally forced all other expansion slot standards off of motherboards. Almost all motherboards today only have PCIe expansion slots. However, some products designed for markets that rely heavily on old hardware continue to produce motherboards that support dated expansion slots.

PCIe has seen numerous upgrades, with PCIe Gen 5 now entering the market. The bandwidth of the PCIe bus has quadrupled with each generation, enabling the PCIe bus to carry a lot of data very quickly. Given their high bandwidth requirements, current graphics cards can connect to it perfectly. High-speed SSDs can also be used with the PCIe bus and, in some situations, PCIe expansion slots. Four 16x PCIe slots will be present on an ATX motherboard from the contemporary era. There might, however, be a number of smaller ones as well. Not all 166 logical PCIe lanes are connected to all physical 16x PCIe slots.

2.5. Power Supply and Cooling Systems

An electrical device known as a power supply provides electricity to an electrical load. A power supply's primary function is to transform electrical current from a source into the proper voltage, current, and frequency needed to drive a load. Because of this, power supplies are sometimes known as electric power converters. While some power supplies are integrated into the load appliances they power, others are independent standalone pieces of equipment. Power supply used in desktop computers and consumer electronics devices are examples of the latter. Power supply used in desktop computers and consumer electronics devices are examples of the latter.

Additional tasks that power supplies may carry out include power-factor correction, limiting the amount of current the load draws to safe levels, cutting off the current in the event of an electrical fault, power conditioning to stop electronic noise or voltage surges from reaching the load, and storing energy so it can keep the load powered even if the source of power is temporarily interrupted (uninterruptible power supply).

All power supplies have one or more power output or rail connections that send current to the load and at least one power input connection that accepts energy in the form of electric current from a source. The power source could be an electrical outlet, a generator, an alternator, a solar power converter, a fuel cell, a battery, the electrical power grid, or another power source. Although some power supplies use wireless energy transfer to power their loads without wires connections, the input and output are typically hardwired circuit connections. For purposes like external monitoring and control, some power supplies also have different kinds of inputs and outputs.

Chapter 3: Software Foundations

Software Foundations usually refers to a section of a book or course syllabus that explores the basic ideas and tenets of software development. It is a fundamental cornerstone for comprehending the creation, writing, and upkeep of software. The following major subjects are frequently covered in this chapter:

- **Programming Languages:** Overview of the syntax and semantics of programming languages. An overview of well-known programming languages including Python, Java, C++, and JavaScript may be found in this section.
- **Data Types and Variables:** Basic data types (such as integers, strings, and floats) are explained, as well as how variables are used to store and manipulate data in a program.
- **Control Structures**: The flow of an application's execution is determined by control structures like loops (for, while) and conditional statements (if-else).
- **Functions and Methods**: Introduction to functions and methods, which are reusable code blocks that carry out particular tasks. The definition of a function, its parameters, and return values are possible topics.
- **Data Structures**: Overview of data structures, including dictionaries, sets, arrays, and lists, and how they are used to manage and organize data.
- **Object Oriented Programming (OOP):** Introduction to the basics of object-oriented programming (OOP), such as classes, objects, inheritance, and polymorphism. This section may examine how OOP is applied to software models of real-world issues.
- **Error Handling:** A description of programming mistakes

and exceptions, including try-catch blocks and error messages.

- **Debugging:** Code troubleshooting and debugging methods, including the use of debugging tools and techniques for finding and resolving faults.
- **Testing and Quality Assurance:** Software testing approaches, such as unit testing, integration testing, and acceptance testing, are discussed in the context of testing and quality assurance. The significance of good code and best practices may also be discussed in this section.
- **Version Control:** An introduction to concepts like repositories, commits, branches, and merging as well as version control systems like Git. Code management and collaboration require version control.
- **Software Development Life Cycle (SDLC):** Overview of the phases in the Software Development Life Cycle (SDLC), from requirements gathering and design to coding, testing, and deployment. Various SDLC models, including Agile and Waterfall, may be introduced in this section.
- **Software Development Tools:** Understanding of fundamental software development tools, such as code editors, package managers, and integrated development environments (IDEs).
- **Documentation:** Emphasis is placed on the value of good, organized documentation in software development. This covers API documentation, code comments, and documentation generators.
- **Software Architecture:** Introduction to the fundamentals of software architecture, including design patterns, separation of responsibilities, and modularity.
- **Ethical and Legal Consideration:** Discussion of the duties

that software developers have in terms of ethics and the law, including topics like cybersecurity, privacy, and intellectual property.

- **Software Development Best Practices:** Introduction to the best principles for producing secure, scalable, and maintainable code in software development. Code review procedures and style guidelines are two examples of this.

Software Foundations is to give readers and students a solid foundation in the fundamental ideas and abilities required for software development. It helps people lay a strong foundation for a career in the industry and acts as the starting point for more complex topics in programming and software engineering.

3.1. Operating Systems: Types and Functions

In order to execute programs and provide a user-friendly interface, operating systems (OS) are essential software elements that manage and control computer hardware and software resources. They come in numerous varieties, each with unique features and uses.

The main categories of operating systems and their purposes are as follows:

3.1.1. **Operating Systems for a Single User or Single Task:** These fundamental operating systems are created for contexts with a single user and a single task. They only permit one person to access the computer at once and execute a single application.

Examples: MS-DOS and other early personal computer operating systems.

3.1.2. Operating Systems for a Single User and Multiple Tasks: By using these operating systems, numerous programs or tasks can be run at once by a single user. They control CPU time-sharing so they can quickly transition between tasks.

Examples include Linux, macOS, and Microsoft Windows.

3.1.3. Operating Systems for Multiple Users: Multi-user operating systems enable numerous users to operate simultaneously on a single computer. To safeguard user data and processes, they offer user authentication, resource allocation, and security.

Examples include mainframe operating systems like IBM z/OS, UNIX, and Linux server distributions.

3.1.4. RTOS: Real-Time Operating Systems: RTOS are made for systems that need quick and reliable responses. They are utilized in a variety of settings, including robots, auto controls, and medical equipment.

Examples include FreeRTOS, QNX, and VxWorks.

3.1.5. Network Operating Systems (NOS): The purpose of NOS is to manage and coordinate network services and resources. In a networked setting, they make it possible for file sharing, printer access, user authentication, and centralized administration.

Examples include Linux server distributions, Windows Server, and Novell NetWare.

3.1.6. Embedded Operating Systems: Function: Lightweight, specialized operating systems known as embedded operating systems are utilized in embedded systems, including consumer electronics, IoT devices, and smartphones. They are created for particular hardware and jobs.

Examples include Android (for smartphones), Embedded Linux (for the Internet of Things), and various real-time embedded OS.

3.1.7. Operating Systems for Mobile Devices: Function: Touch-based interfaces, app ecosystems, and features like battery management are all part of mobile OS, which are designed specifically for smartphones and tablets. They enable connectivity and support for mobile applications.

Examples include Android, iOS (Apple), and Huawei's HarmonyOS.

3.1.8. Functions of the Operating System:

Operating systems, irrespective of kind, carry out a number of crucial tasks, including

- **Process Management:** The operating system (OS) controls how programs are run, allots CPU time, and promotes effective multitasking.
- **Memory Management:** It manages and distributes memory resources to processes, including RAM and virtual memory.
- **File System Management:** The OS controls the creation, deletion, and access of files, preserving the integrity of the

file system.

- **Device Management**: Ensures proper interaction with hardware elements like drives, printers, and network adapters by managing device communication and resource allocation.
- **User Interface:** To communicate with a computer, operating systems offer user interfaces, such as command-line interfaces (CLI) or graphical user interfaces (GUI).
- **Security and Access Control:** To safeguard data and resources, OS incorporates user authentication, authorization, and access control.
- **Networking:** In networked contexts, the operating system (OS) controls network configurations and facilitates device connectivity.
- **Logging and Error Handling:** It keeps track of system errors, records events, and outputs error messages for troubleshooting.
- **System Updates and Maintenance:** To maintain the system secure and up-to-date, OS facilitates software updates, patches, and system maintenance.
- **Resource Monitoring:** In order to improve system performance, it keeps track of how much CPU, memory, and disk space are being used.

An essential part of contemporary computing, operating systems serve as a bridge between hardware and software, facilitating resource management and allowing for seamless interaction. An operating system's kind and features depend on the particular computing environment and needs of the system it supports.

3.2. System Software vs. Application Software

The two main software categories known as system software and application software each have a specific function within the computing ecosystem.

The distinctions between the two are broken down as follows:

3.2.1. Purpose:

- **System Software:** This kind of software is in charge of overseeing and directing the hardware of the computer. It guarantees the proper operation of the computer system and offers a platform for running application software. It is necessary for the fundamental functions of the computer.
- **Application Software:** Is created to carry out particular functions or applications for users. It is designed to meet a range of user needs, including gaming, graphic design, and online browsing as well as word processing. System software is necessary for the operation of application software.

Examples: Operating systems like Windows, macOS, and Linux are examples of system software, as are device drivers that make hardware like printers, graphics cards, and input devices compatible with computers.

Microsoft Word, Adobe Photoshop, Mozilla Firefox, and video games like Minecraft are all examples of application software. These are applications that consumers utilize directly to carry out particular actions or tasks.

3.2.2. Functionality:

- **System Software's** main duties include managing hardware resources, offering a user interface, and ensuring that

different software programs can execute on the computer. The management of files, memory, and hardware connection are among the duties it undertakes.
- **Application Software**: This program has a narrow scope. It is intended to carry out specific duties or tasks, such as data analysis, document editing, image editing, or web browsing.

3.2.3. User Engagement:

- **System Software:** Users often interact with system software indirectly through the operating system's user interface. Users could make advantage of the OS's built-in file explorer, for instance.
- **Application software**: To complete their tasks, users work directly with application software. Within these programs, they launch applications and create, edit, and save files.

3.2.4. Installation and Updates:

- **System software:** When you buy a computer, it typically comes pre-installed. Operating system updates are frequently issued on a recurring basis by the OS manufacturer and are used to upgrade system software.
- **Application Software**: Depending on their demands, users must install application software separately. The user is required to install application software updates, which are normally given by the program manufacturers.

3.2.5. Customizability:

- **System software**: System software customization options are typically constrained to system settings and configurations. Screen resolution, battery settings, and security options are among the configurations that users can select.

- **Application software:** Has a wide range of settings and features that can be specifically adapted to a user's tastes or needs.

In conclusion, the responsibilities that system software and application software play in the computing environment are distinct. While application software delivers specific functionality to satisfy diverse user needs, system software provides the framework for the computer's operation. Together, the two forms of software allow users to complete tasks.

3.3. Programming Languages and Compilers

Compilers and programming languages are critical elements of software development. They each perform a unique but connected role in the creation and execution of computer programs.

Let's examine the definitions of programming languages, compilers, and how they interact:

3.2.1. Programming Languages

- **Definition:** A codified set of rules and syntax known as a programming language is used to give instructions to a computer on how to carry out particular activities or processes.
- **Purpose:** Developers can communicate their methods and instructions in a structured, human-readable manner using programming languages.
- **Types:** There are many different programming languages, and each has advantages and uses. There are numerous popular programming languages, such as Python, Java, C++, JavaScript, and Ruby.
- **Features:**
    - *Syntax:* The grammar and conventions for writing code in programming languages are specific. When a piece of code doesn't follow these guidelines, syntax errors happen.
    - *Semantics:* The semantics of a language specify how statements and expressions should be used.
    - Programming languages with different levels of abstraction enable developers to work at varied levels of complexity and depth.
    - *Libraries:* Programming languages frequently

include libraries or frameworks that offer pre-built tools and methods to make simple jobs faster.
    - *Development:* To construct software programs, scripts, or systems, developers write code in a programming language.

1. **Compilers:**

- **Definition:** A compiler is a specialized software tool that converts source code written in a programming language into intermediate code or machine code so that a computer may execute it.
- **Purpose:** A compiler's main function is to translate high-level, human-readable programming code into low-level machine code that the computer's CPU can understand.
- **Process:** There are often numerous steps in compilation:
- **Lexical Analysis:** The words and symbols that make up the source code are called tokens.
- *Syntax Analysis:* The compiler validates the syntax and organization of the code.
- Some compilers generate intermediate code, which is a representation of the code.
- *Coding efficiency* may be improved by optimization.
- Code generation: The compiler creates the finished executable file or line of machine code.
- **Advantages:** Programs operate more effectively thanks to the highly optimized machine code produced by compilers.
- Code can run unaltered on several hardware systems thanks to the level of abstraction provided by compilation.
- **Examples:** The GNU Compiler Collection (GCC) for C/C++, Java's javac, Python's CPython (which includes a bytecode compiler), and many others are examples of common compilers.

1. **Programming Languages and Compilers: Their**

Relationship

- Developers can convey their goals and logic in a human-readable manner using programming languages.
- On the other hand, compilers convert this high-level code into a form that the CPU of a computer can understand.
- Compilers and interpreter systems that translate programming languages' code into machine code might vary.
- Programming language selection can have an impact on variables like readability of the code, speed of development, and performance, while compilers have an impact on how effectively the code is performed.

In conclusion, programmers write code using programming languages, and compilers are the instruments that turn this code into commands that can be carried out by machines. Together, they make up the essential elements of software development and give programmers the ability to design a wide variety of systems and applications.

3.4. Virtual Machines and Emulators

Emulators and *Virtual Machines* (VMs) are two technologies used in the field of computing to execute software or full operating systems on hardware or platforms other than those for which they were designed. However, they have unique qualities and slightly different functions. Let's look more closely at virtual machines and emulators:

3.4.1. VMs (virtual machines):

- **Definition:** A virtual machine simulates a physical computer using software. It enables the concurrent use of several operating systems (guest OS) on a single physical machine (host OS). Every VM functions as if it were a separate computer.
- **Purpose:** Creating isolated environments for applications or services, server consolidation, development, and testing are the main uses of virtual machines (VMs). They offer a method for running various OS instances on a single physical server.
- **Hypervisor:** A hypervisor, which is a layer of software or hardware that regulates the distribution of physical resources to each VM, manages virtual machines. Hypervisors like VMware, Hyper-V, and VirtualBox are examples.
- **Performance:** Because they use the same hardware resources and run on the host OS, VMs are typically more effective than emulators. However, because of resource allocation, there can still be some performance overhead.
- **Examples:** For desktop use, prominent virtual machine programs include VMware Workstation and Oracle VirtualBox, while Microsoft Hyper-V and VMware vSphere are frequently used for server virtualization.

3.4.2. Emulators:

- **Definition:** An emulator is a piece of software or hardware that enables one computer system, known as the host, to mimic the operations of another computer system, known as the guest. It duplicates the target system's full architecture, down to the CPU, RAM, and peripherals.
- **Purpose:** The main function of emulators is to execute programs or games made for one platform on a different one. Emulators can be used, for instance, to test mobile apps on desktop computers or to run vintage console games on contemporary PCs.
- **Performance**: Because they must translate instructions and replicate hardware components, emulators are typically less efficient than virtual machines (VMs). This can result in significant performance overhead.
- **Examples:** You can play Nintendo GameCube and Wii games on a PC using the Dolphin emulator. You may run Android apps on a Windows or macOS computer using an emulator for Android, such as Bluestacks.

3.4.3. Key Variations:

- Emulators are focused on simulating the behaviour of certain hardware or platforms, whereas VMs are made to run whole operating systems.
- Since virtual machines run on the same hardware as the host operating system, they are more effective and provide greater performance than emulators, which can have a high overhead.
- While VMs are used for server consolidation, testing, and building isolated environments, emulators are frequently used for gaming and app development (such as testing

mobile apps on a PC).

- Emulators can run software from a foreign platform without modification, whereas VMs frequently need a guest OS that is compatible.

In conclusion, emulators and virtual machines are tools that let software execute in many contexts or environments. While emulators are made to run software or games from one platform on another, virtual machines (VMs) are best for running several operating systems on a single host. The specific use case and needs will determine which one is best.

3.4.4. Key differences between Virtual Machines (VMs) and Emulators

Aspect	Virtual Machines (VMs)	Emulators
Purpose	VMs are primarily used to create multiple isolated virtual instances of an operating system on a single physical host, allowing for efficient resource allocation and management.	Emulators are used to replicate the behavior of one computer system (the target) on a different one (the host), often for testing or running software from one platform on another
Virtualization Level	VMs provide full system virtualization, allowing the execution of multiple guest operating systems on a host system without modifying the guest OS.	Emulators provide software-based, often CPU-level emulation, simulating the entire hardware and software environment of the target system.
Performance	VMs generally have better performance than emulators, as they run directly on the host hardware and share resources efficiently.	Emulators tend to be slower due to the overhead of translating and emulating hardware instructions and system calls.
Hardware Interaction	VMs interact directly with the host's hardware, which may require hardware virtualization support (e.g., Intel VT-x, AMD-V) for improved performance.	Emulators simulate hardware interactions in software, translating and emulating instructions to mimic the behavior of the target hardware.
Isolation	VMs offer strong isolation between virtual instances, ensuring that issues in one VM do not affect others.	Emulators provide isolation but may have limitations in terms of isolating software components due to the nature of emulation.
Resource Overhead	VMs have some resource overhead but are generally efficient in resource usage and	Emulators have higher resource overhead due to the translation and emulation of hardware

	can provide near-native performance.	instructions, resulting in reduced performance.
Operating Systems	VMs can run multiple guest operating systems, including different versions of Windows, Linux, macOS, and others.	Emulators can run various guest operating systems, including those for different architectures or legacy systems.
Use Cases	VMs are commonly used for server consolidation, software development, testing, and creating isolated environments for applications.	Emulators are used for cross-platform development, running legacy software, and simulating hardware environments for debugging and testing.
Examples	• VMware Workstation • VirtualBox • Microsoft Hyper-V	• QEMU (Quick Emulator) • Android Emulator for running Android apps on non-Android platforms • Apple's Rosetta 2 for running x86 apps on Apple Silicon (ARM) Macs

Figure 2: Key differences between Virtual Machines (VMs) and Emulators

Note: Virtual Machines (VMs) provide efficient and isolated environments for running multiple operating systems on a single host, while Emulators replicate the behaviour of a target hardware and software environment for cross-platform development, testing, or running legacy software. VMs are generally more performance-efficient and suitable for running a wide range of operating systems, while emulators are useful for simulating specific hardware and software environments.

Chapter 4: Computer Architecture

4.1. Von Neumann Architecture

The Von Neumann architecture, commonly referred to as the *Von Neumann model* or the *Von Neumann machine*, is a fundamental framework for computer architecture that underpins the construction and functionality of contemporary digital computers. John von Neumann, a mathematician and computer scientist, first proposed it in the 1940s, and it has since been included into the design of the majority of general-purpose computers. Several crucial characteristics define the Von Neumann architecture:

4.1.1. CPU: Central Processing Unit: The primary component in charge of carrying out calculations and carrying out commands is the CPU. It consists of a control unit (CU) for fetching, decoding, and executing instructions as well as an arithmetic and logic unit (ALU) for mathematical calculations.

4.1.2. Memory: The Von Neumann architecture stores both data and program instructions in a single, integrated memory system. The CPU may access particular regions to read or write data and instructions because this memory is normally structured into addresses.

4.1.3. Computer Program Counter: The CPU's program counter is a register that maintains track of the memory address of the following instruction. As each instruction is fetched and carried out, it is automatically increased.

4.1.4. Instruction Set: The CPU sequentially fetches instructions from memory after they have been put there. Each instruction represents a particular action, such as arithmetic, data transfer, or control flow, and is encoded in a particular format.

4.1.5. Data Path: Data can be transferred between memory, the CPU, and other components thanks to a network of channels and registers called the data path. ALU processing and memory storage of processed data are all possible.

4.1.6. Control Unit: The control unit coordinates the operation of the CPU, interprets and decodes instructions, and manages the data flow between components. It retrieves instructions from the program counter and, when necessary, guides the ALU and data stream.

4.1.7. Concept of Stored-Programs: The idea of a stored program is one of the cornerstones of the Von Neumann architecture. In this concept, data and program instructions are both kept in memory, and program instructions can be handled just like other types of data. This adaptability enables the development of flexible, programmable computers.

4.1.8. Execution in Sequence: According to the program counter, instructions are carried out in a sequential order, one after the other. The Von Neumann architecture is characterized by this linear execution of instructions.

4.1.9. Cycle of Fetch-Decode-Execute: The "Fetch-Decode-Execute Cycle," which governs how the Von Neumann architecture functions, is a continuous cycle. An instruction is read from memory, its operation is determined by decoding it, it is then carried out, and the program counter is increased to proceed on to the next instruction.

Since its creation, the Von Neumann architecture has served as the foundation for the majority of computer designs. It offers a straightforward and practical architecture for general-purpose computing, but it also has drawbacks, such as the potential for memory access bottlenecks.

The Von Neumann architecture's essential principles have been preserved while a number of architectural changes and upgrades have been made to lessen these restrictions.

4.2. Harvard Architecture

The Harvard architecture is a type of computer architecture that divides the processing and storing of data and instructions into various memory units. It bears the name of the Harvard Mark I computer, which was created in the 1940s at Harvard University. The employment of distinct memory units for program instructions and data, which enables simultaneous access to both types of information, is the distinguishing feature of the Harvard architecture.

The key characteristics and benefits of Harvard architecture are as follows:

4.2.1. Separate Memory for Instructions and Data: In a computer with a Harvard architecture, there are two distinct memory systems: one for storing data (*data memory or data cache*) and another for storing program instructions (*instruction memory or code memory*). Conflicts between fetching instructions and data access are eliminated by this division.

4.2.2. Parallel Access: The Harvard architecture enables the CPU to fetch an instruction while concurrently carrying out data operations by allowing simultaneous access to both instruction and data memory. Execution could be quicker and more effective as a result of this parallelism.

4.2.3. Faster Instruction Fetch: Fetching an instruction from memory in a conventional computer architecture could entail waiting for earlier data accesses to finish. Instruction fetch delays brought on by data conflicts are avoided in the Harvard design since instruction and data access are separate.

4.2.4. Streamlined Control Unit: Because a Harvard architecture computer doesn't require complicated systems to handle instruction and data conflicts, its control unit is frequently simpler than a Von Neumann architecture computer's.

4.2.5. A Coherent Cache: Since data and instructions can be cached individually, the Harvard architecture can simplify cache management. This can lessen potential conflicts and increase cache coherency.

4.2.6. Common Use Cases: In embedded systems, microcontrollers, and digital signal processors (DSPs), where speed and efficiency are crucial, Harvard design is frequently used. These systems frequently need easy access to data and software instructions.

4.2.7. Examples: The Atmel AVR, Microchip PIC, and ARM Cortex-M series are just a few of the microcontroller families that utilise the Harvard design. The Harvard architecture is also used by various DSP processors, such as the Texas Instruments TMS320 family.

Despite its benefits, the Harvard architecture has several drawbacks as well:

- Separate instruction and data memories demand additional physical memory space, which can raise the price and complexity.
- Given that data and instructions are stored in multiple memory locations, programming for the Harvard architecture may call for specific considerations.
- When instruction and data memory are separate, there is sometimes a risk that one memory area will go unused.

In conclusion, the Harvard architecture is a type of computer architecture that divides the memory used for instructions from the memory used for data, enabling simultaneous access to both. In embedded systems and specialized processors, where speed and efficiency are crucial, it is frequently employed.

4.2.8. List of differences between Von Neumann Architecture and the Harvard architecture

Aspect	Von Neumann Architecture	Harvard Architecture
Instruction and Data Memory	Von Neumann uses a single memory unit for both instructions and data, sharing a common memory bus.	Harvard has separate memory units for instructions and data, each with its dedicated memory bus.
Fetch-Execute Cycle	In Von Neumann, the processor alternates between fetching instructions and accessing data from the same memory.	Harvard allows simultaneous fetching of instructions and data, as they are stored in separate memory units.
Instruction and Data Paths	Von Neumann uses a single data path for both instructions and data processing, making it more flexible but potentially slower.	Harvard has separate data paths for instructions and data, which can improve performance by reducing data access conflicts.
Instruction Set	Von Neumann typically uses a single, unified instruction set architecture (ISA) for both instructions and data operations.	Harvard may use separate ISAs for instructions and data, allowing for specialized instruction sets optimized for specific tasks.
Complexity	Von Neumann architecture is generally simpler in terms of hardware design, making it more cost-effective and easier to implement.	Harvard architecture can be more complex due to the separate data paths and memory units, potentially requiring more hardware resources.
Instruction and Data Access	Von Neumann architecture can lead to potential bottlenecks when	Harvard architecture mitigates bottlenecks by allowing concurrent access to instructions and data,

	simultaneous instruction and data access occur, affecting performance.	potentially improving performance.
Program Execution Speed	Von Neumann may be slower for certain tasks that involve frequent instruction and data access due to memory contention.	Harvard can offer improved execution speed for tasks that benefit from simultaneous instruction and data access, such as digital signal processing (DSP) applications.
Examples	Most general-purpose computers, including PCs and laptops, use a Von Neumann architecture.	Embedded systems like microcontrollers often use a Harvard architecture to optimize performance for specific tasks.
Advantages	• Simplicity in design and lower cost • Flexibility in program execution.	• Improved performance for specific tasks • Reduced contention for memory access.
Disadvantages	• Potential bottlenecks in memory access. • Slower execution for certain tasks.	• Complex hardware design may be more costly • Less flexibility for program execution.

Figure 3: List of differences between Von Neumann Architecture and the Harvard Architecture

Note: The Von Neumann architecture uses a single memory unit for both instructions and data, while the Harvard architecture employs separate memory units and data paths for instructions and data. Harvard architecture can provide improved performance in certain scenarios but may be more complex and costly to implement. Von Neumann architecture is simpler and offers flexibility in program execution but can suffer from memory access bottlenecks. The choice between the two architectures depends on the specific requirements of the computing system and its intended use.

4.3. RISC vs. CISC Architectures

Each of the two opposing computer architecture design philosophies—RISC (Reduced Instruction Set Computer) and CISC (Complex Instruction Set Computer)—has advantages and disadvantages. These architectural strategies have different ways of handling instructions and structuring the instruction set. The following are some of the main distinctions between RISC and CISC architectures:

4.3.1. Reduced Instruction Set Computer, or RISC

4.3.1.1. Set of instructions: RISC architectures often only have a tiny fixed number of instructions and have a simpler and reduced instruction set. These guidelines are intended to be straightforward and carry out fundamental functions.

4.3.1.2. Complexity: RISC processors place an emphasis on consistency and simplicity in the execution of instructions. Simpler instructions are constructed from a series of more complex ones. RISC processors are simpler to develop and optimize because of this.

4.3.1.3. Execution of Instructions: Each instruction is completed in a single clock cycle in RISC architectures, which results in a more consistent and predictable instruction execution time. A process that frequently involves moving data between registers and memory prior to completing calculations is known as a "load-store" operation.

- **Registers:** A lot of general-purpose registers are often present on RISC processors, allowing for quick access to data. There is less need to routinely access memory because register-to-register operations are frequent.
- **Pipelining:** Deep instruction pipelines are a common characteristic of RISC processors, enabling the concurrent execution of instructions. High throughput and enhanced

performance may arise from this.

- **Storage Access:** For memory access, RISC systems rely on load and store instructions. This can make memory accesses simpler, but it might also mean that more instructions are required to complete some tasks.
- **Examples:** Examples of RISC architectures utilized in different computing devices, such as mobile devices, embedded systems, and servers, include ARM, MIPS, and PowerPC.
- **Compound Instruction Set Computer (CISC):**
- **Instruction Set:** Instructions that may perform several operations with just one instruction are part of the more comprehensive and complicated instruction set found in CISC architectures. These guidelines are frequently adjusted for certain jobs.
- **Complexity:** High-level abstractions and a reduction in the quantity of instructions required to complete tasks are the goals of CISC processors. Memory access, mathematical computations, and control flow instructions are examples of complex instructions.
- **Execution of Instructions:** Instructions may be executed by CISC processors over a range of clock cycles, which makes the execution time less predictable. Microcode routines might be used in some instructions.
- **Registers:** Comparing CISC CPUs to RISC architectures, fewer registers are typically included. As a result, retrieving operands from memory may need to happen more frequently.
- **Pipelining:** Because CISC processors may have shorter instruction pipelines, the amount of instruction-level parallelism may be constrained, and throughput may not be as high as with RISC architectures.

- **Memory Access**: Instructions that directly access memory are frequently found in CISC designs, which can be convenient for programmers but may result in less effective memory utilization.
- **Examples:** Examples of CISC architectures frequently used in personal computers and servers include Intel x86 and AMD x86-64 (also known as IA-32 and x86-64).

Essential Factors: Due to their simplicity and power economy, RISC architectures typically succeed in energy-efficient, embedded, and mobile applications.

- In general-purpose computing, when backward compatibility and a broad variety of complicated operations are crucial, CISC architectures are ideally suited.
- The distinctions between RISC and CISC processors are sometimes blurred by the inclusion of features from both architectures. These processors are frequently referred to as CISC-RISC hybrids or RISC-VLIW (Very Long Instruction Word) processors.

The specific needs of the intended application and the processor's design objectives determine whether to use RISC or CISC architecture. Many contemporary processors include elements from both architectures to strike a compromise between performance, compatibility, and power efficiency.

4.4. Pipelining and Parallel Processing

The performance and effectiveness of processors and computer systems are enhanced through the use of parallel processing and pipelining in computer architecture. While there are some parallels between them in terms of segmenting tasks into smaller pieces and carrying them out concurrently, they each have unique properties and uses.

Let's investigate each of these ideas:

4.4.1. Pipelining:

- **Definition:** Pipelining is an architectural approach that divides the execution of commands or tasks into several stages, each of which is carried out simultaneously. Instructions pass through the pipeline one after another, with each stage performing a particular operation on the instruction.
- **Stages:** A pipelined processor often has numerous phases, including fetching instructions, decoding instructions, executing them, accessing memory, and writing back. Each step carries out a particular operation on the directive or assignment.
- **Cross-over of Tasks:** A pipeline is a series of steps where numerous instructions or jobs are handled concurrently. The system's throughput and overall performance are enhanced by this task overlap.
- **Advantages:** By decreasing the amount of time needed to complete a series of instructions or operations, pipelining can result in considerable performance benefits. It works very well for enhancing ILP (instruction-level parallelism).
- **Example:** The way a CPU executes instructions is a prime illustration of pipelining. A new instruction can be

retrieved while the preceding one is being decoded and executed because the fetch-decode-execute cycle is separated into several stages that run concurrently.

4.4.2. Parallel Processing

- **Definition:** To increase system throughput and performance, parallel processing involves the simultaneous execution of many activities or instructions. It is a more comprehensive idea that includes multiple methods for carrying out tasks concurrently.
- **Various Parallel Processing Methods**
- **Task-level Parallelism**: The simultaneous execution of multiple independent tasks or processes on various processors or cores.
- **Data-Level Parallelism**: Using SIMD (Single Instruction, several Data) instructions, several data pieces are processed simultaneously.
- **Instruction-Level Parallelism**: To increase throughput, instructions are carried out simultaneously by a pipelined processor.
- **Advantages:** For tasks that can be parallelized, parallel processing can result in considerable speedups and performance gains. Large-scale data processing and computationally demanding tasks benefit especially from its effectiveness.
- **Examples:** GPUs, multicore CPUs, and multiprocessor systems are some examples of hardware that makes use of parallel processing to carry out numerous tasks at once.
- Software developers can create applications that make use of parallel processing resources by using frameworks for parallel programming like OpenMP, MPI, and CUDA.

4.4.3. Key Variations:

- Parallel processing entails running many activities simultaneously, whereas pipelining is a specialized technique inside a processor architecture that requires breaking down a single job into multiple steps.
- By overlapping the execution steps of a single task or instruction stream, pipelining primarily aims to increase throughput. The term "parallel processing" refers to a wider range of methods for carrying out several tasks concurrently.
- While parallel processing might entail many processors or cores working on various tasks or data at once, pipelining is better suited for enhancing instruction-level parallelism (ILP) within a CPU.

In conclusion, parallel processing and pipelining are two strategies for enhancing processor and computer system performance. Pipelining focuses on improving the performance of a particular job, whereas parallel processing involves running several activities at once to increase the throughput and performance of the system as a whole. The specific needs of the computing task and the hardware resources available determine which technique should be used.

4.4.4. Key differences between RISC and CISC

Aspect	-RISC (Reduced Instruction Set Computer)	CISC (Complex Instruction Set Computer)
Philosophy	**RISC** processors use a simplified instruction set with a focus on executing instructions quickly and efficiently.	**CISC** processors employ a larger and more complex instruction set with diverse and powerful instructions.
Instruction Set	RISC architectures have a limited set of simple instructions, typically executing one operation per instruction.	CISC architectures have a rich instruction set with complex and multi-step instructions that can perform multiple operations in a single instruction.
Complexity of Instructions	RISC instructions are generally simple and uniform in execution, making them faster to decode and execute.	CISC instructions can be complex, requiring multiple clock cycles to decode and execute.
Pipelining	RISC processors often implement pipelining for improved instruction throughput, with a fixed number of stages.	CISC processors may have longer and variable instruction execution times, making pipelining more challenging to implement.
Hardware Design	RISC CPUs have simpler hardware design, which can result in smaller chip sizes, reduced power consumption, and cost-effectiveness.	CISC CPUs can be more complex in hardware design, potentially requiring more resources and power.
Performance per Clock Cycle	RISC architectures tend to have a higher performance per clock cycle (IPC) due to the simplicity of instructions.	CISC architectures may have a lower IPC due to complex instructions, but they may compensate with fewer instructions per program.

Memory Usage	RISC architectures may require more memory due to the need for additional instructions to achieve desired functionality.	CISC architectures may use memory more efficiently due to complex instructions that perform multiple tasks.
Code Size	RISC code tends to be larger, as more instructions are needed to accomplish tasks.	CISC code can be more compact, as fewer instructions are required for the same task.
Program Execution	RISC processors execute programs by breaking them into simpler instructions and optimizing instruction-level parallelism (ILP).	CISC processors may execute programs by relying on complex instructions, which can reduce the need for extensive ILP optimization.
Compiler Dependence	RISC architectures depend more on optimizing compilers to extract performance from simple instructions.	CISC architectures can rely on hardware features to execute complex instructions efficiently, reducing the compiler's role.
Examples	• ARM (Advanced RISC Machines) • MIPS (Microprocessor without Interlocked Pipeline Stages) • PowerPC	• x86 (Intel and AMD processors) • Intel 80486 (an example of early CISC design) • VAX (Digital Equipment Corporation)
Common Usage	RISC architectures are commonly used in mobile devices, embedded systems, and high-performance	CISC architectures are prevalent in personal computers, servers, and desktop computing.

computing (HPC) clusters.

Figure 4: Key differences between RISC and CISC

Note: RISC architectures prioritize simplicity, fast execution, and reduced hardware complexity, resulting in efficient execution of simple instructions. CISC architectures, on the other hand, offer a rich instruction set with complex instructions that can perform multiple tasks in a single instruction, potentially reducing code size but with more hardware complexity. The choice between RISC and CISC depends on the specific requirements and use cases of the computing system.

4.5. Multiprocessor Systems

Computer systems with numerous central processing units (CPUs) or processor cores that cooperate to carry out activities and carry out commands are referred to as multiprocessor systems, multiprocessor computers, or multiprocessor architectures. These systems are made to increase processing power, concurrency, and performance. Multiple configurations of multiprocessor systems are available, and they are utilized in a variety of applications, including servers, supercomputers, desktop computers, and embedded systems. A few crucial features of multiprocessor systems are as follows:

4.5.1. Multiple CPUs or Cores: The existence of many CPUs or processor cores is what distinguishes a multiprocessor system. Each core or CPU has the ability to independently carry out its own set of instructions.

4.5.2. **Parallel Executions:** Multiple CPUs or cores can work on various aspects of a task concurrently because multiprocessor systems are built to execute tasks in parallel. The performance of the entire system can be greatly enhanced by this parallelism.

4.5.3. Different Multiprocessor System Types: Symmetric Multiprocessing (SMP): SMP systems use identical CPUs or cores that share the same main memory and peripherals. Every CPU has equal access to system resources and can carry out any task.

4.5.4. Asymmetric Multiprocessing (AMP): In AMP systems, one CPU or core is designated as the "master" and is in charge of running the computer system, while the other CPUs or cores serve as "slave" processors and are used to perform particular functions. A lot of real-time systems employ AMP.

4.5.5. Clustered Systems: Are made up of a number of independent computers (nodes) connected by a network. The nodes can collaborate on distributed computing tasks and each one may have its own set of processors and memory.

4.5.6. Non-Uniform Memory Access, or NUMA: Refers to systems with numerous processor nodes and local memory on each of them. Even while all CPUs can access all memory, local memory access is faster than remote memory access, resulting in uneven memory access times.

4.5.7. Multicore Processors: A large number of contemporary CPUs combine several processor cores into a single chip. These multicore CPUs can be thought of as single-chip multiprocessor systems.

4.5.8. Applications:

- Servers and data centres to manage concurrent user requests and data processing are two applications where multiprocessor systems are used.

- Supercomputers for high-performance simulations in science and engineering. The use of desktop computers to improve performance and multitasking in activities like gaming and content creation.
- Multiple real-time jobs can be handled by embedded systems, such as industrial controls and automobile electronics.

4.5.9. Support for Software: Software must be developed or adjusted to take use of parallelism if multiprocessor computers are to be used to their full potential. This could entail synchronization techniques, parallel algorithms, and multithreading.

4.5.10. Scalability: By adding more CPUs or cores, multiprocessor systems may frequently be expanded to handle increasing computational demands.

4.5.11. Challenges: Multiprocessor system design and programming can be challenging due to factors including load balancing, inter- communication, and cache coherence. Testing and debugging can be more difficult as well.

4.5.12. Gains in Performance: The speed improvements brought about by multiprocessor systems depend on various elements, including the kind of applications being used, the effectiveness of parallelization, and the system's scalability. Multiple processors provide different advantages for different applications.

In conclusion, multiprocessor systems are computer architectures that use many CPUs or cores to carry out tasks concurrently and increase system performance. They are a crucial part of contemporary computer infrastructure and are available in a variety of configurations, each of which is appropriate for particular applications and workloads.

Chapter 5: Storage Systems

5.1. Introduction

In computing environments, storage systems are essential because they give users the ability to reliably and efficiently store and retrieve data. This chapter examines a number of storage system-related topics, such as storage designs, data management strategies, and storage devices.

5.1.1. Storage Devices

- **HDDs (Hard Disk Drives):** The most popular non-volatile storage devices in use right now are HDDs. They are made up of read/write heads, rotating platters, and a spindle motor. The chapter discusses their organization, functionality, and distinguishing features.
- **SSDs: Solid-State Drives:** SSDs don't have any moving parts and store data on NAND flash memory. Although they tend to cost more per gigabyte, they are speedier and more reliable than HDDs. The benefits and drawbacks of SSD technology are covered in this section.
- **Optical Storage:** Laser technology is employed by optical storage media like DVDs and Blu-ray discs to read and write data. The section goes through the fundamentals of optical storage and some of its uses.
- **Tape Drives:** For backup and long-term archive storage, tape drives are employed. The benefits of tape storage, the sequential access aspect of it, and its applications are covered in this section.

5.1.2. Storage Architectures

- **Reliable Array of Independent Disks (RAID):** RAID

configurations can be used to improve performance, data protection, or a mix of the two. The various RAID levels, their advantages, and trade-offs are explained in this chapter.

- **SANs (Storage Area Networks):** Dedicated networks called SANs give users quick access to consolidated storage resources. The SAN architecture, elements, and use cases are covered in this section.
- **NAS: Network-Attached Storage:** Over a network, NAS systems offer file-level storage. The NAS architecture, functionality, and deployment scenarios are explored in this section.
- **Systems for Distributed Files:** Large volumes of data can be stored and managed across several nodes or servers using distributed file systems like HDFS (Hadoop Distributed File System). The notion of distributed file systems and their benefits are introduced in this chapter.

5.1.3. Management of Data

- **File Management:** Software called file systems controls how data is stored and arranged on storage devices. File system ideas, structures, and popular file systems including NTFS, ext4, and FAT32 are explained in this chapter.
- **Deduplication of data:** By removing duplicate data, data deduplication techniques demand less storage space. The benefits of deduplication techniques are covered in this section.
- **Backup And Recovery Of Data**: Strategies for data backup are crucial for data safety. Disaster recovery planning, backup types, and strategies are covered in this chapter.
- **Virtualized Storage:** To create a more adaptable and scalable storage environment, storage virtualization isolates

physical storage resources. The principles and technologies of storage virtualization are examined in this section.

A crucial part of the infrastructure for modern computing is storage systems. To better assist readers in selecting and managing storage solutions, this chapter offers insights into the various storage devices, architectures, and data management strategies.

5.1. Hard Disk Drives (HDDs) and Solid State Drives (SSDs)

Computers and other electronic devices use two different types of storage devices: hard disk drives (HDDs) and solid state drives (SSDs). Although they have the same basic function of storing and retrieving data, their technological, performance, and physical qualities are very different. The following chart contrasts HDDs vs SSDs:

5.1.1. HDDs (Hard Disk Drives):

5.1.1.1. Technology: HDDs store data on magnetic platters that have been coated in a magnetic substance. A moving actuator arm equipped with read/write heads that can reach particular tracks on the spinning platters is used to read and write data.

5.1.1.2. Speed And Performance: The physical restrictions of spinning platters cause HDDs to generally operate more slowly than SSDs. Latency is influenced by seek time, which is the length of time it takes for the read/write heads to find the desired data.

5.1.1.3. Durability: Since HDDs feature moving components like spinning disks and read/write heads, they are more prone to being physically harmed by shock or vibration. Data loss might result from sudden hits.

5.1.1.4. Heat and Noise: HDDs generate heat and noise during operation as a result of their moving parts. This can be taken into account in settings where minimal heat and noise production are required.

5.1.1.5. Capacity: In comparison to SSDs, HDDs often provide greater storage capabilities at a lower cost per gigabyte. They frequently serve as mass storage solutions.

5.1.1.6. Consumption of Energy: Because the spinning disks and actuator motor require power to run, HDDs use more energy than SSDs. Laptop batteries and those of other portable electronics may be affected by this.

5.1.1.7. Longevity: HDDs have a limited shelf life, and the mechanical parts might deteriorate with time, perhaps resulting in drive failures. Important data must be backed up.

5.1.2. SSDs: Solid State Drives

5.1.2.1. Technology: NAND flash memory chips are used by SSDs to store data. In an SSD, there are no moving parts. Data is kept in memory cells and can be electrically read and written.

5.1.2.2. Speed and Performance: SSDs outpace HDDs in terms of speed. Higher data transmission speeds, lower latency, and quicker data access times are all features they offer. As a result, the system responds more quickly overall and applications load and boot up more quickly.

5.1.2.3. Durability: Because they don't have moving parts that could be destroyed, SSDs are more resilient than HDDs. They are more durable in portable devices and less susceptible to physical shock and vibration.

5.1.2.4. Heat and Noise: SSDs produce extremely little heat and are silent when in use. Cooler and quieter computing environments may result from this.

5.1.2.5. Capacity: SSDs come in a variety of capacities, including those appropriate for high-performance storage and common computing activities. In contrast to HDDs, they are typically more expensive per GB.

5.1.2.6. Consumption of Energy: SSDs use less energy than HDDs, which can increase the battery life of laptops and the overall durability of the device.

5.1.2.7. Longevity: Comparatively speaking, SSDs last longer than HDDs. Modern SSDs use wear-levelling techniques and overprovisioning to increase the lifespan of NAND flash memory cells, which can deteriorate over time.

5.1.2.8. Which Is the Best Choice?

Your particular needs will determine whether you choose an HDD or an SSD:

- An SSD is a superior option if you need high-speed performance, reliability, and a responsive computing environment.
- An HDD could be a better option if you require a high storage capacity at a low cost per gigabyte, particularly for mass data storage and backups.
- Some users choose to combine the two, employing an SSD for the operating system and commonly used programs (*to benefit from speed*) and an HDD for additional storage capacity (*to benefit from affordability*).

In the end, your choice should be based on your needs for storage, financial constraints, and performance expectations.

5.2. Optical Storage Media

Laser technology is used to read and write data on optical storage medium. They are frequently employed for the distribution and archiving of digital data in a variety of formats. On a reflective surface, usually a disc, optical storage medium work by encoding data as a succession of pits and lands. These patterns are read by a laser beam, and the presence or absence of a hole or piece of land correlates to binary 0s and 1s. Several popular kinds of optical storage medium are listed below:

5.2.1. CDs: Compact Discs

CDs were among the first types of optical storage, and they are still in use today for the storing of audio and data.

- **Compact Disc, or CD-ROM** read-only CDs that include pre-recorded data, such as software, music, or video, are referred to as read-only memory.
- **Compact Disc Recordable (CD-R)**: Writable CDs that allow users to record data only once; however, once recorded, the data cannot be erased or overwritten.
- **Compact Disc Re-Writable** (CD-RW): Reusable CDs that enable numerous data writing, erasure, and rewriting operations.

5.2.2. DVDs (Digital Versatile Discs):

DVDs have a larger storage capacity than CDs and are frequently used to store data, software, and movies.

- **Read-only DVDs** having pre-recorded data are known as DVD-ROMs.
- **Writable DVDs** for one-time recording include DVD-R and DVD+R (*DVD Recordable*).

- **Reusable DVDs** for numerous recordings and erasures include DVD-RW and DVD+RW (*DVD Re-Writable*).

5.2.3. BDs, or Blu-ray Discs:

High-definition movies and massive data storage are frequently stored on Blu-ray discs since they have a larger storage capacity than DVDs.

- **Blu-ray disc**, or BD-ROM Read-Only Memory (*ROM*) Blank Blu-ray discs.
- **BD-R** (*Blu-ray Disc Recordable*): Blu-ray discs that can be written to once for recording.
- **Reusable Blu-ray discs** for numerous recordings and erasures are known as BD-RE (*Blu-ray Disc Re-Writable*).

5.2.4. Archives on discs

- **Archival CDs** are made to preserve data over time. They live longer and are more resistant to the effects of the environment.
- Examples include *M-DISCs*, which etch data onto the disc for long-term stability using a specific recording layer.

5.2.5. Mini Discs and CDs/DVDs on business cards: Smaller optical discs, such as Mini CDs and Business Card CDs/DVDs, were created for specific applications, such as the storage of small amounts of data and the creation of promotional materials.

5.2.6. UHD Blu-ray: 4K and 8K ultra-high quality movies and other content are stored on Ultra High quality Blu-ray discs (UHD Blu-ray). Durability, immunity to magnetic interference, and the capacity to produce read-only discs for distribution are all benefits of optical storage media. However, compared to other storage technologies like hard drives and solid-state drives, they have limitations in terms of storage capacity. For some applications, optical media are being increasingly supplanted by digital downloads and streaming, but they are still useful for archiving and for some physical media requirements.

5.2.7. Key differences between HDD, SSD, Optical Drive, and Tape Drive

Aspect	HDD (Hard Disk Drive)	SSD (Solid-State Drive)	Optical Drive	Tape Drive
Storage Medium	HDDs store data on spinning magnetic disks with read/write heads that access data on the disk's surface.	SSDs use NAND flash memory chips to store data electronically without any moving parts.	Optical drives use optical discs, such as CDs, DVDs, or Blu-ray discs, to read and write data using lasers.	Tape drives use magnetic tape as the storage medium, where data is written sequentially along the tape.
Data Access Speed	HDDs have relatively slower data access speeds due to the mechanical movement of the read/write heads and spinning disks.	SSDs offer significantly faster data access speeds, as there are no moving parts, resulting in low latency.	Optical drives have moderate data access speeds, with read and write times depending on the optical disc type.	Tape drives have slower data access speeds, as data is accessed sequentially along the tape, and random access is limited.
Durability and Reliability	HDDs are susceptible to physical shock, vibration, and wear and tear due to their mechanical components, making them	SSDs are more durable because they lack moving parts, making them resistant to shock and vibration.	Optical drives are moderately durable but can be sensitive to scratches and dust on optical discs.	Tape drives are relatively durable and resistant to physical damage, making them suitable for long-term

	less durable.			data storage.
Noise and Heat Generation	HDDs produce noise and heat due to the spinning disks and moving read/write heads, which may require cooling solutions.	SSDs are silent and generate very little heat because they have no moving parts, contributing to a quieter and cooler environment.	Optical drives can produce noise when reading or writing discs, and they generate moderate heat.	Tape drives are generally quiet and generate minimal heat during operation.
Power Consumption	HDDs consume more power due to the mechanical components, resulting in higher energy consumption.	SSDs consume less power, making them more energy-efficient and suitable for laptops and portable devices.	Optical drives consume moderate power during operation, but power consumption is relatively low during standby.	Tape drives consume moderate power when reading or writing data
Form Factor and Portability	HDDs are available in various form factors, including 2.5-inch and 3.5-inch drives, and can be portable but less compact.	SSDs come in compact form factors, including M.2 and NVMe drives, making them highly portable and suitable for slim devices.	Optical drives have standard form factors, and portable versions are available for laptops and external use.	Tape drives are not as portable and are typically used for backup and archival purposes in data centers.
Data Density	HDDs offer	SSDs offer	Optical discs	Tape drives

and Capacity	higher data density and capacity for the cost, making them suitable for large-scale data storage.	lower data density compared to HDDs but provide high-speed access to data, ideal for performance-critical applications.	have limited data density and capacity compared to HDDs and SSDs, suitable for smaller data storage needs.	can offer high data density and capacity, making them suitable for long-term archival storage of large datasets.
Cost per Gigabyte	HDDs generally offer a lower cost per gigabyte of storage compared to SSDs, making them cost-effective for mass storage.	SSDs have a higher cost per gigabyte compared to HDDs but provide faster performance and durability.	Optical discs are relatively inexpensive on a per-disc basis, but the cost per gigabyte can be higher for larger storage needs.	Tape drives can offer a low cost per gigabyte for long-term storage but may require initial hardware investment
Data Lifespan and Retention	HDDs have a finite lifespan and may fail due to mechanical wear over time. Data retention is typically several years.	SSDs have a limited number of write cycles, but modern SSDs can have a long lifespan. Data retention can be several years.	Optical discs have a relatively long data retention lifespan, often exceeding a decade or more under proper storage conditions.	Tape drives are designed for long-term data retention, with data lifespans of decades or even longer when stored properly.

Copyright: Patrick Mukosha (2023

Figure 5: Key differences between HDD, SSD, Optical Drive, and Tape Drive

Note: HDDs and SSDs are commonly used for general data storage, with SSDs offering superior speed and durability but at a higher cost per gigabyte. Optical drives are used for reading and writing optical discs, and tape drives are suitable for long-term data archival and backup, offering high capacity and data retention. The choice depends on the specific storage requirements and use cases.

5.3. RAID (Redundant Array of Independent Disks)

RAID, short for Redundant Array of Independent Disks, is a technology used in computer storage to increase data dependability, availability, and performance. By integrating several physical hard drives into a single logical unit, RAID is able to achieve these objectives. There are different RAID levels, and each one uses a different technique for data mirroring, data striping, or both.

Some of the most popular RAID levels are listed below:

5.3.1. RAID 0 (Striping): Having data spread across numerous drives allows for simultaneous reading from and writing to multiple disks, which can enhance performance. There is no fault tolerance or redundancy; if a drive fails, all data is gone. Frequently used for applications that require high speed where data backup is not the main priority.

5.3.2. RAID 1 (Mirroring): On two or more drives, data is duplicated. All drives in the array receive a mirror copy of every write operation. Great data redundancy; in the event of a drive failure, the data is still accessible via the mirror drive(s). Although read performance can be enhanced, write performance might not reap the same rewards.

5.3.3. RAID 5 (Striping using Parity): Similar to RAID 0, data is striped across several disks, but parity information is used. Brings performance and redundancy together in a positive way. Can withstand a single drive failing without losing any data.

5.3.4. RAID 6 (Striping with Dual Parity): Similar to RAID 5, but with dual parity, so it can tolerate the simultaneous failure of two drives. Provides strong data redundancy but may not write as quickly as RAID 5.

5.3.5. RAID 10 (Also Known As Mirror-Striping or RAID 1+0): Combines striping and mirroring (RAID 0 and RAID 0 respectively) to increase performance and redundancy. A minimum of four drives are necessary. Can endure numerous drive failures, depending on how each drive fails inside each mirrored pair.

5.3.6. Arrays 50 and 60: These are RAID 5 and RAID 0 combinations (RAID 50) or RAID 6 and RAID 0 combinations (RAID 60).

For bigger arrays, strike a compromise between performance and redundancy.

The selection of a RAID level is based on the particular needs of a system, such as the required level of redundancy, performance requirements, and financial limitations. Hot-swapping capabilities, which let you replace faulty disks without shutting down the system, are another feature that some RAID controllers offer.

5.4. Cloud Storage and Object Storage

Two types of data storage services that are frequently utilized in cloud computing environments are cloud storage and object storage. While they both have the same function of cloud data storage, they differ in terms of their traits and potential applications.

5.4.1. Cloud Storage: Various storage options provided by cloud providers fall under the broad category of "cloud storage." Both block storage and file storage are a part of it. The following are some essential attributes of cloud storage:

a. **File Storage:** Much like conventional on-premises file servers, cloud storage providers frequently offer a file-based storage system that enables you to store and retrieve files and directories.
b. **Block Storage:** You can construct and manage raw storage volumes that can be connected to virtual machines using the block storage services that cloud providers provide. These volumes are often used to store block-level data such as operating system files, databases, and other data. Examples include Azure Managed Disks, Google Persistent Disks, and Amazon EBS.
c. **Mounting:** You can frequently mount storage volumes or file shares to virtual machines using cloud storage, which makes it simple to use and gain access to the storage within your cloud architecture.
d. **Scalability:** To meet fluctuating storage requirements, cloud storage may be quickly scaled up or down. The capacity of your storage resources can be changed as needed.

e. **Performance:** While file storage is appropriate for a wide range of use cases, including file sharing among several users, block storage is primarily geared for high-performance applications.
f. **Pricing:** Depending on the cloud provider, there may be several pricing tiers and alternatives for cloud storage. Typically, you pay for the capacity you use over time.

1. **Object Storage:**

A particular kind of cloud storage called object storage is designed specifically for archiving and recovering unstructured data like backups, log files, photos, videos, and documents. The following characteristics define it:

a. **Data Objects:** In object storage, data is kept as objects, each of which has metadata and a special identifier (often a URL or key). These objects, which come in different sizes, are frequently accessed using HTTP or other RESTful APIs.
b. **Scalability:** Object storage systems can store enormous volumes of data and are extremely scalable, making them ideal for large data and archive applications.
c. **Durability and Availability**: High durability and availability are priorities in the design of object storage systems. To maintain data resilience, they frequently replicate data across several data centres or locations.
d. **Simple APIs:** Developers can easily include object storage into their applications since access to object storage is often made possible through simple APIs.
e. **Cost-Effective:** Compared to conventional file or block storage systems, object storage is frequently more affordable for storing huge volumes of data.
f. **Use Cases:** Object storage is frequently used as a backend

for web applications that demand scalable and dependable data storage, content delivery, media storage, and backup and disaster recovery.

Popular object storage systems include Azure Blob Storage, Google Cloud Storage, and Amazon S3 (Simple Storage Service).

5.4.3. Key differences between Cloud Storage and Object Storage

Aspect	Cloud Storage	Object Storage
Data Storage Model	Cloud storage is a broader term that encompasses various storage models, including file storage, block storage, and object storage	Object storage is a specific storage model designed for storing and managing unstructured data as discrete objects, each with a unique identifier.
Data Organisation	Cloud storage may use various hierarchical structures, such as directories and folders, to organize data in a manner similar to traditional file systems.	Object storage uses a flat namespace, where data is organized into a pool of objects, each with its unique identifier (e.g., a unique URL or key).
Data Access Method	Cloud storage supports different access methods, including file-based access (e.g., NFS, SMB), block-level access (e.g., iSCSI), and RESTful APIs for object access.	Object storage primarily uses HTTP/HTTPS-based RESTful APIs (e.g., Amazon S3, Azure Blob Storage) for data access and manipulation.
Meta Data and Tags	Cloud storage systems often include metadata and tagging capabilities to provide additional information about files and objects.	Object storage heavily relies on metadata, which is stored with each object, enabling rich metadata-based searching and indexing.
Scalability	Cloud storage can scale vertically or horizontally based on the specific storage model in use (e.g., adding more disks or nodes).	Object storage is highly scalable and designed for massive scalability across distributed storage clusters, suitable for handling vast amounts of data.
Data	Cloud storage typically offers	Object storage systems are

Durability	data durability guarantees through redundancy and backup mechanisms, depending on the service provider	designed for high data durability, often using data replication across multiple locations or erasure coding techniques.
Use Cases	Cloud storage can be used for various purposes, including traditional file storage, database storage, and virtual machine disks.	Object storage is ideal for storing and managing unstructured data types, such as images, videos, backups, logs, and archives
Pricing Model	Cloud storage pricing varies based on the storage model used (e.g., pay-as-you-go, tiered storage, or provisioned capacity) and the amount of data stored.	Object storage pricing is typically based on data storage volume, data transfer, and the number of requests (e.g., GET, PUT, DELETE) made to the object storage service.
Data Consistency	Cloud storage models may offer strong consistency guarantees for file or block storage but can vary in consistency depending on the implementation.	Object storage systems often provide eventual consistency, where changes to objects may take some time to propagate across distributed storage nodes.
Examples	• Amazon EBS (Elastic Block Store) • Azure File Storage • Google Cloud Persistent Disks	• Amazon S3 (Simple Storage Service) • Azure Blob Storage • Google Cloud Storage

Copyright: Patrick Mukosha (2023

Figure 6: Key differences between Cloud Storage and Object Storage

Note: Cloud Storage encompasses various storage models, including file, block, and object storage, while Object Storage is a specific storage model designed for managing unstructured data as discrete objects. Object storage relies on flat namespaces, uses RESTful APIs, and is highly scalable, making it well-suited for storing large volumes of unstructured data like images, videos, and backups. Cloud storage models, on the other hand, may include file and block storage in addition to object storage, catering to a broader range of use cases.

In conclusion, while both object storage and cloud storage fulfil data storage requirements in cloud computing, they are tailored to distinct data types and use scenarios. A wider range of storage services, such as file and block storage, are included in cloud storage, whereas object storage is made especially for the scalable and economical storage of unstructured data objects. Your individual storage needs and application requirements will determine which option you choose.

Chapter 6: Networking and Communication

6.1. Introduction to Networking

The process of linking computers and other devices in order to share resources and information is known as networking. Modern computing and communication systems depend on it fundamentally to let devices to communicate and share data via a variety of mediums, including wires, cables, and wireless connections. The internet, intranets, LANs, WANs, and other networks require networking in order to function. When learning about networking, it's important to comprehend the following ideas:

6.1.1 Network: A network is a group of connected devices (such as computers, servers, routers, switches, printers, etc.) that allows for resource sharing and communication. A home network is a small-scale example of a network, while the internet is an enormous network.

6.1.2 Protocols: Within a network, protocols define the guidelines by which data is sent over and received. They specify the structure of data packets, how to handle errors, and the protocols that devices must adhere to in order to interact efficiently. Network protocols include TCP/IP, HTTP, and Ethernet as examples.

6.1.3 Internet: A global network of interconnected networks, the internet. It enables information sharing and communication amongst gadgets everywhere. It is dependent on a set of protocols that have been established, like the Transmission Control Protocol (TCP) and Internet Protocol (IP).

6.1.4 LAN (Local Area Network): A LAN is a type of network that only covers a small area, like a campus, workplace, or home. LANs, which frequently make use of Ethernet and Wi-Fi, link up nearby devices.

6.1.5 WAN (Wide Area Network): A WAN connects LANs or other networks over considerable distances and often covers a greater geographic area. The internet is a very large WAN. Leased lines, MPLS, and VPNs are all examples of WAN technology.

6.1.6 IP Address: Each device on a network is given an IP address, which is a special numerical identification. It enables devices to find and connect with one another. IPv4 (32-bit) and IPv6 (128-bit) are the two primary forms of IP addresses; the latter was created to address the shortage of IPv4 addresses.

6.1.7 DNS (Domain Name System): DNS is a system that converts domain names that are easily recognizable by humans (such as www.example.com) into IP addresses that computers may use to find one another on the internet. As a distributed directory, it helps the internet.

6.1.8 Router: A router is a networking tool that links various networks and directs traffic between them. It is essential in figuring out the route that data follows from its source to its destination.

6.1.9 Switch: In Ethernet LANs, switches are used to link devices that are part of the same network segment. Data is forwarded to the intended location using MAC addresses while operating at the data connection layer (Layer 2).

6.1.10 Firewall: A firewall is a security tool or piece of software that regulates network traffic entering and leaving an organization in accordance with previously specified security standards. It assists in defending networks from illegal access and online dangers.

6.1.11 Bandwidth: The ability of a network connection to transmit data is referred to as bandwidth. Bits per second (bps) are the usual unit of measurement, and more bandwidth enables faster data transport.

6.1.12 Topology: A network's topology is its logical or physical organization. The topologies star, bus, ring, and mesh are frequently used.

6.1.13 Security: Protecting a network and its data against unauthorized access, threats, and vulnerabilities is the goal of network security. This covers procedures like intrusion detection, authentication, and encryption.

Anyone who works with computers, IT experts, and anybody who want to understand the intricacies of contemporary communication and connectivity need to understand these basic networking concepts. Keeping up with the most recent innovations is essential because networking is constantly evolving due to technological breakthroughs.

6.2. Network Topologies and Protocols

The process of linking computers and other devices in order to share resources and information is known as networking. Modern computing and communication systems depend on it fundamentally to let devices to communicate and share data via a variety of mediums, including wires, cables, and wireless connections. The internet, intranets, LANs, WANs, and other networks require networking in order to function.

When learning about networking, it's important to comprehend the following ideas:

6.2.1. **Network:** A network is a group of connected devices (such as computers, servers, routers, switches, printers, etc.) that allows for resource sharing and communication. A home network is a small-scale example of a network, while the internet is an enormous network.

6.2.2. **Protocols:** Within a network, protocols define the guidelines by which data is sent over and received. They specify the structure of data packets, how to handle errors, and the protocols that devices must adhere to in order to interact efficiently. Network protocols include TCP/IP, HTTP, and Ethernet as examples.

6.2.3. **Internet:** A global network of interconnected networks, the internet. It enables information sharing and communication amongst gadgets everywhere. It is dependent on a set of protocols that have been established, like the Transmission Control Protocol (TCP) and Internet Protocol (IP).

6.2.4. **LAN (Local Area Network):** A LAN is a type of network that only covers a small area, like a campus, workplace, or home. LANs, which frequently make use of Ethernet and Wi-Fi, link up nearby devices.

6.2.5. **WAN (Wide Area Network):** A WAN connects LANs or other networks over considerable distances and often covers a greater geographic area. The internet is a very large WAN. Leased lines, MPLS, and VPNs are all examples of WAN technology.

6.2.6. **IP Address:** Each device on a network is given an IP address, which is a special numerical identification. It enables devices to find and connect with one another. IPv4 (32-bit) and IPv6 (128-bit) are the two primary forms of IP addresses; the latter was created to address the shortage of IPv4 addresses.

6.2.7. **DNS (Domain Name System):** DNS is a system that converts domain names that are easily recognizable by humans (such as www.example.com) into IP addresses that computers may use to find one another on the internet. As a distributed directory, it helps the internet.

6.2.8. **Router:** A router is a networking tool that links various networks and directs traffic between them. It is essential in figuring out the route that data follows from its source to its destination.

6.2.9. **Switch:** In Ethernet LANs, switches are used to link devices that are part of the same network segment. Data is forwarded to the intended location using MAC addresses while operating at the data connection layer (Layer 2).

6.2.10. **Firewall:** A firewall is a security tool or piece of software that regulates network traffic entering and leaving an organization in accordance with previously specified security standards. It assists in defending networks from illegal access and online dangers.

6.2.11. **Bandwidth:** The ability of a network connection to transmit data is referred to as bandwidth. Bits per second (bps) are the usual unit of measurement, and more bandwidth enables faster data transport.

6.2.12. **Topology:** A network's topology is its logical or physical organization. The topologies star, bus, ring, and mesh are frequently used.

6.2.13. **Security**: Protecting a network and its data against unauthorized access, threats, and vulnerabilities is the goal of network security. This covers procedures like intrusion detection, authentication, and encryption.

Anyone who works with computers, IT experts, and anybody who want to understand the intricacies of contemporary communication and connectivity need to understand these basic networking concepts. Keeping up with the most recent innovations is essential because networking is constantly evolving due to technological breakthroughs.

6.3. TCP/IP and OSI Models

Two conceptual frameworks are used to comprehend and standardize how various networking protocols and technologies interact in computer networks: the TCP/IP model and the OSI (Open Systems Interconnection) model. Each layer in both models has its own distinct functions and is made up of several levels. Let's investigate each model in greater depth:

6.3.1. Open Systems Interconnection Model (OSI Model): The International Organization for Standardization (ISO) created the OSI model as a conceptual framework to regulate the appearance and performance of networking protocols and systems. It offers a thorough understanding of how network communication functions and is made up of seven levels, each of which is in charge of particular duties:

a. **Physical Layer:** The physical medium and hardware elements like cables, switches, and network interface cards (NICs) are dealt with in the physical layer. Voltage levels, cable types, and data transmission rates are all defined.
b. **Data Layer:** Establishing a trustworthy link between two nodes that are directly connected falls under the purview of the data link layer. It manages addressing of devices on the same network segment as well as error detection and correction. At this layer, Wi-Fi and Ethernet function.
c. **Network Layer**: The network layer is in charge of directing data packets between various networks or subnets. It chooses the most efficient route for data to take to get to its destination using logical addressing, like IP addresses. At this layer, the Internet Protocol (IP) functions.

d. **Transport Layer:** The transport layer guarantees end-to-end device connectivity. It manages data segmentation and reassembly, flow management, and error recovery. Examples of transport layer protocols include the Transmission Control Protocol (TCP) and User Datagram Protocol (UDP).
e. **Session Layer:** The session layer establishes and controls communication sessions among devices. It takes care of session creation, upkeep, and termination.
f. **Presentation Layer**: Data translation, encryption, and compression are all handled by the presentation layer. It makes sure that the data is presented in a way that is clear to both the sender and the recipient.
g. **Application Layer:** The application layer directly offers user applications network services. It contains protocols for file transfers, SMTP for email, and HTTP for web browsing.

1. Transmission Control Protocol/Internet Protocol (TCP/IP) Model

The Internet protocol suite, commonly referred to as the TCP/IP model, is a more condensed model that was created to define the protocols and technologies utilized on the internet. There are four layers to it:

a. **Network Interface Layer:** This layer is equivalent to the OSI model's physical and data link levels. The physical medium and device addressing on the local network segment are covered.
b. **Internet Layer:** The OSI network layer's counterpart is the internet layer. It is in charge of employing logical addressing, usually IP addressing, to route messages between various networks.

c. **Transport Layer:** This layer manages end-to-end communication and contains both the TCP and UDP protocols, much like the OSI model.
d. **Application Layer:** The OSI presentation and application layers' functions are combined in the TCP/IP model's application layer. It covers numerous services and protocols necessary for application-level internet communication.
e. **Key Differences:**

- The TCP/IP model is more streamlined than the OSI model, which has seven layers, and only four layers.
- The TCP/IP model represents the actual protocol suite used on the internet, whereas the OSI model was created as a conceptual foundation.
- The TCP/IP model is more useful for comprehending internet protocols and technologies, whereas the OSI model offers a more thorough and in-depth view of networking ideas.

The two theories are complementary and both are helpful for comprehending network communication. In order to troubleshoot and build networks, network specialists frequently combine both approaches.

6.3.3. Key differences between the TCP/IP model and the OSI model

Aspect	TCP/IP (Transmission Control Protocol/ Internet Protocol) model	OSI (Open Systems Interconnection) model:
Number of layers	The TCP/IP model has four layers: Application, Transport, Internet, and Network Interface.	The OSI model has seven layers: Application, Presentation, Session, Transport, Network, Data Link, and Physical.
Development Origins	Developed by the U.S. Department of Defense and evolved from real-world Internet protocols.	Developed as a conceptual framework by the International Organization for Standardization (ISO) for standardizing network protocols.
Commonly Used Protocols	TCP/IP includes widely used protocols like TCP, UDP, IP, HTTP, SMTP, FTP, and DNS.	OSI is more of a theoretical model and does not specify specific protocols.
Adoption and Prevalence	TCP/IP is the foundational model for the modern internet and is widely used in practice.	OSI is primarily used as a conceptual reference but has limited practical implementation.
Layering Philosophy	TCP/IP adopts a pragmatic approach, with fewer layers that often have overlapping functionality.	OSI follows a strict layering philosophy, with clear separation of responsibilities between layers.
Encapsulation Terminology	TCP/IP uses different terminology for encapsulation, including segments (Transport),	OSI uses consistent terminology throughout, with data units referred to

	packets (Internet), and frames (Network Interface).	as PDUs (Protocol Data Units) at each layer.
Standards Organisation	TCP/IP standards are maintained by various organizations, including the Internet Engineering Task Force (IETF).	OSI standards are maintained by the International Organization for Standardization (ISO).
Model Complexity	TCP/IP is considered simpler due to its reduced number of layers, which can lead to more efficient implementations.	OSI is more complex due to its seven-layer structure and its emphasis on conceptual clarity.
Compatibility with Internet	TCP/IP was designed for and is the foundation of the internet, making it seamlessly compatible.	OSI is not inherently tied to the internet and requires translation or mapping to work with TCP/IP-based networks.
Teaching and Reference Model	TCP/IP is often used as a practical reference model for teaching networking due to its real-world relevance.	OSI is used as a theoretical model for teaching networking concepts and principles.
Layer Correspondence	In the TCP/IP model, the Transport layer often combines functions that are separated into multiple layers in the OSI model, such as the Transport and Session layers.	In the OSI model, each layer has distinct and well-defined responsibilities, resulting in a clear separation of functions.

Figure 7: Key differences between the TCP/IP model and the OSI model

Note: The TCP/IP model is a practical and widely used model that forms the basis of the internet and includes well-defined protocols. In contrast, the OSI model is more of a theoretical framework for understanding network concepts and layers but has limited practical implementation in real-world networks

6.4. Local Area Networks (LANs) and Wide Area Networks (WANs)

There are two main categories of computer networks: LANs and WANs. Each is created for a particular function and operates at a different size. Let's examine the main traits and distinctions between LANs and WANs:

6.4.1. Local Area Network (LAN)

a. **Scope:** LANs are often used within a single building, office, or school because they are intended for relatively narrow geographic areas. They provide services to a constrained space's consumers and gadgets.
b. **Topology:** The star, bus, ring, and mesh topologies are frequently used in LANs. Common LAN technologies for cable and wireless connections, respectively, are Ethernet and Wi-Fi.
c. **Ownership:** LANs are frequently owned, controlled, and managed by a single entity, like a business or educational institution.
d. **Data Transmission Rate:** LANs often provide fast data transfer rates, frequently in the gigabits per second (Gbps) range or higher. They are suitable for activities like file sharing, printer access, and intranet services because they are optimized for local communication and resource sharing.
e. **Cost:** Due to their smaller size than WANs, LANs are considerably less expensive to install and operate.
f. **Security:** Since LANs are often contained within a regulated physical location, they are seen as being relatively secure. Firewalls, access control, and data encryption are all examples of security mechanisms.

g. *Examples:* Common LAN deployments include data centres, college networks, residential networks, and office LANs.

Workstations in a LAN

Figure 8: Workstations in a Local Area Network (LAN)

Note: Workstations are specialist computers used for jobs that call for specialized hardware and high-performance computation.

6.4.2. Wide Area Network (WAN)

a. **Scope:** Greater geographic areas, such as towns, nations, continents, or even the entire world, are covered by WANs. Over considerable distances, they link LANs and other networks.
b. **Topology:** Point-to-point connections, leased lines, and different network equipment like routers and switches are frequently used in WANs to build intricate, interconnected networks. An international WAN is the internet itself.
c. **Ownership:** WANs may be privately owned by businesses, such as the network of a large firm, or they may be a component of the public internet infrastructure.

d. **Data Transmission Rate:** Depending on the underlying technologies and the distance between network nodes, WANs may have different data transfer speeds. WAN technologies include things like satellite linkages, MPLS (Multiprotocol Label Switching) networks, and internet connections.

e. **Cost:** Due to the requirement for long-distance communication infrastructure, such as dedicated lines or subscriptions, WAN deployment and maintenance expenses are often greater.

f. **Security:** Due to the fact that data in WANs flows across public networks and could be vulnerable to numerous threats, security issues are raised. To improve WAN security, VPNs (Virtual Private Networks), encryption, and secure tunnelling protocols are frequently utilized.

g. *Examples:* Examples of WANs include the internet, international corporate networks, telecommunications networks, and cross-continental data linkages.

In conclusion, LANs are localized networks that provide high-speed communication in constrained spaces and are created for small to medium-sized locations. Typically, a single company owns and operates them. In contrast, WANs connect LANs and other networks over greater distances, incur higher costs, and frequently rely on existing public infrastructure. Making decisions on network design and management requires an understanding of the differences between LANs and WANs.

6.4.3. Key differences between LAN and WAN

Aspect	LAN (Local Area Network)	WAN (Wide Area Network)
Scope	LAN covers a limited geographical area, typically within a single building or campus	WAN spans a broad geographical area, connecting LANs or other networks across cities, countries, or continents
Size	LANs are smaller in size, often serving a single organization, office, or campus.	WANs are larger in size and can connect multiple LANs, offices, or data centers over extended distances.
Ownership	LANs are usually owned and controlled by a single organization or entity, such as a company or institution.	WANs can be privately owned, but they often involve leased or public infrastructure, and multiple organizations may share WAN resources.
Topologies	LANs commonly use bus, ring, star, or mesh topologies, depending on the network's design and requirements.	WANs often use point-to-point or hub-and-spoke topologies to interconnect remote locations efficiently.
Data Transfer Speed	LANs typically offer higher data transfer speeds, often measured in gigabits per second (Gbps) or faster.	WANs may have lower data transfer speeds compared to LANs, depending on the technology and distance involved.
Latency	LANs have lower latency, as data travels shorter distances within the network, resulting in minimal delays.	WANs introduce higher latency due to data traversing longer distances and potentially passing through multiple network devices.
Protocols	LANs commonly use Ethernet and Wi-Fi protocols for local data communication within the	WANs may use various protocols, including IP (Internet Protocol), MPLS

	network.	(Multiprotocol Label Switching), and SONET (Synchronous Optical Networking).
Cost	LAN setup and maintenance costs are typically lower, as they cover smaller areas and use less complex equipment.	WANs often involve higher setup and operational costs, including expenses for leased lines or dedicated connections.
Reliability	LANs tend to be more reliable and have lower failure rates due to their smaller size and localized maintenance.	WANs can be less reliable due to their larger scale and exposure to external factors like weather and physical infrastructure issues.
Security	LANs are considered more secure because they are contained within a single organization's premises, making it easier to control access and implement security measures.	WANs require additional security measures and may involve encryption, VPNs (Virtual Private Networks), and firewalls to protect data during long-distance transmission.
Examples	• Local office networks within a company • Home Wi-Fi networks	• The internet itself is a global WAN • Corporate networks connecting branch offices across different cities or countries

Copyright: Patrick Mukosha (2023

Figure 9: Key differences between LAN and WAN

Note: LANs are smaller, localized networks designed for data communication within a limited geographical area, typically belonging to a single organization. WANs, on the other hand, cover larger geographical areas and are used to connect multiple LANs or remote locations, often involving leased or public infrastructure and higher latency. The choice between LAN and WAN depends on the scale and requirements of the network.

6.5. Wireless Networking and Mobile Communication

Mobile connectivity and wireless data transfer are made possible by two closely related technologies called wireless networking and mobile communication. They have altered how we obtain information, communicate, and conduct business. Let's examine the following ideas:

6.5.1. Wireless Networking

The technology and infrastructure known as wireless networking enable devices to connect to a network without the use of actual cable connections. It offers ease, mobility, and adaptability in a range of settings.

Key characteristics of wireless networking include:

a. **Wireless Access Points (APs):** Devices like computers, cell phones, and tablets can connect to a local network wirelessly via wireless local area networks, which employ Wi-Fi technology. Homes, workplaces, public venues, and educational institutions all frequently have WLANs.
b. **Wi-Fi Access Points (APs):** In order to connect wireless devices to a wired network, wireless access points transmit Wi-Fi signals. A wireless mesh network, which is sometimes referred to as multiple APs creating a wireless network that covers a bigger region, is possible.
c. **Wi-Fi Standards:** The performance and capabilities of wireless networks, including data transfer rates and range, are defined by Wi-Fi standards like 802.11n, 802.11ac, and 802.11ax.
d. **Wireless Security**: To prevent unwanted access, wireless networks must include security features including encryption (WPA2/WPA3), strong passwords, and access

limits.

e. **Applications:** Internet access, online gaming, video streaming, IoT device connectivity, and mobile applications that depend on wireless data transmission are all made possible via wireless networking.

   1. **Mobile Communication:** Technologies that enable people to communicate and access data while moving around are referred to as mobile communication. It has a strong connection to wireless networks and portable electronics like smartphones and tablets.

Mobile communication essentials include:

a. **Mobile Networks**: Cellular networks, which offer wireless phone and data services to mobile devices, are the foundation of mobile communication. These networks are segmented into cells, and a cell tower (base station) serves each cell.
b. **Mobile Technology:** Voice conversations, text messages, and data access are all made possible by the cellular radios found in mobile devices, including smartphones and feature phones. A variety of mobile applications are supported by mobile operating systems including Android and iOS.
c. **4G and 5G Technology:** Cellular technology's 4G (LTE) and 5G generations both provide faster data rates, lower latency, and increased network capacity. Innovations like IoT connection and augmented reality software are anticipated to be made possible with 5G.
d. **Mobile Applications (Apps)**: Mobile apps are software programs created specifically for smartphones and tablets and provide a range of features and services. Platforms for the distribution of apps are offered by app stores, such as the

Apple App Store and Google Play Store.

e. **Mobile Security**: In order to safeguard user data, mobile devices and applications must include security methods including device encryption, app permissions, and biometric authentication.
f. **Mobile Services:** Voice calls, text messaging (SMS and MMS), email, social networking, video conferencing, and mobile internet surfing are all forms of mobile communication.
g. **Roaming:** Mobile users who are roaming can stay connected while on the go by connecting to networks from different service providers, generally at a cost.

Mobile communication and wireless networking have both had a significant impact on enterprises and society. They make it possible to work remotely, do business online, communicate in real time, and access information from almost anywhere. These sectors will be extremely important in determining the direction of connectivity and communication as technology develops further.

6.5.3. Key differences between Wireless Networking and Mobile Communication

Aspect	Wireless Networking	Mobile Communication
Definition	**Wireless Networking** refers to the use of wireless technologies to connect devices and create networks for data exchange.	**Mobile Communication** refers to the transmission of voice and data over wireless networks to enable mobile device communication.
Focus	Wireless networking primarily focuses on creating wireless LANs (Local Area Networks) or WLANs for data connectivity within a specific area.	Mobile communication focuses on providing voice and data services for mobile devices, including smartphones and tablets, while on the move.
Devices Involved	Wireless networking involves various devices, such as routers, access points, laptops, and IoT devices, to establish wireless data connections.	Mobile communication revolves around mobile devices like smartphones, feature phones, and tablets, which connect to cellular networks.
Connectivity Range	Wireless networks typically have limited range, covering specific areas, such as homes, offices, or public hotspots.	Mobile communication provides wireless connectivity over a broader geographic area, often spanning entire cities or regions through cellular towers.
Network Types	Wireless networks can include Wi-Fi, Bluetooth, Zigbee, and other wireless technologies, typically used for LANs and short-range communication.	Mobile communication networks are primarily cellular networks, including 2G, 3G, 4G LTE, and 5G, designed for wide-area wireless communication.
Data Speeds	Wireless networking can offer high data speeds, especially	Mobile communication data speeds vary but may be slower

	with the latest Wi-Fi standards (e.g., Wi-Fi 6), suitable for data-intensive tasks.	than some Wi-Fi networks, with faster speeds achieved on 4G and 5G networks.
Use Cases	Wireless networking is used for local data sharing, internet access, home automation, and connecting IoT devices within a confined area.	Mobile communication is used for voice calls, text messaging, internet access, mobile apps, and location-based services while on the go.
Infrastructure	Wireless networking often relies on fixed infrastructure, including wireless access points or routers, which provide wireless access to devices.	Mobile communication infrastructure includes cellular towers and base stations that cover large geographic areas, connecting mobile devices to the network.
Roaming	Wireless networking typically does not involve device roaming unless moving between different Wi-Fi networks or access points within the same WLAN.	Mobile communication allows for seamless device roaming as users move across different cellular towers and network areas.
Coverage	Wireless networking coverage is confined to the range of access points or hotspots and may have dead zones where connectivity is unavailable.	Mobile communication offers wider coverage, with the network continuously adapting to provide service across a larger area.
Examples	• Home Wi-Fi networks • Public Wi-Fi hotspots	• Mobile phone networks (2G, 3G, 4G, 5G) • Mobile data plans

• Wireless LANs in offices	for smartphones • Mobile messaging apps like WhatsApp

Figure 10: Key differences between Wireless Networking and Mobile Communication

Note: Wireless networking focuses on local wireless data connectivity within specific areas, often utilizing technologies like Wi-Fi for LANs. Mobile communication, on the other hand, provides wireless voice and data services over wide geographic areas, primarily through cellular networks, allowing mobile devices to communicate while on the move. Both play critical roles in modern communication and connectivity.

6.6. Network Topologies and Protocols

In order for data to be structured, sent, and received within a network, network topologies and protocols are crucial elements of computer networks. Let's investigate both ideas:

6.6.1. Network Topologies

The physical or logical organization of links and devices within a network is referred to as network topology. It describes the connections between nodes (such as PCs, servers, routers, switches, etc.). In terms of scalability, fault tolerance, and simplicity of maintenance, different network topologies offer a variety of benefits and drawbacks. Following are a few typical network topologies:

a. **Star Topology**: All devices are linked to a central hub or switch in a star architecture. It is simple to administer and install, and if one device malfunctions, it has no effect on the others. It can be costly to implement, though, and the network could collapse if the central hub fails.
b. **Bus Topology:** All devices in a bus topology are

interconnected by a single central cable. The network can be completely disrupted by a cable break, making it less fault-tolerant than more complex and expensive systems.

c. **Ring Topology:** Each device in a ring topology is connected to exactly two additional devices, forming a circular path. Until it reaches its destination, data moves around the ring in a single direction. Although it can be more difficult to set up and operate, it offers good fault tolerance.
d. **Mesh Topology**: Every device in the network is connected to every other device in a mesh topology. It offers high redundancy and fault tolerance, guaranteeing that data can still find a different path even if one link or device fails. Due to the vast number of connections, scaling in larger networks can be costly and difficult.
e. **Hybrid Topology:** To satisfy particular network requirements, a hybrid topology mixes two or more of the aforementioned topologies. It enables businesses to strike a balance between performance, redundancy, and cost-effectiveness.

6.6.2. Network Protocols

Network protocols are sets of guidelines that specify how data should be formatted, sent through a network, received, and processed. Different systems and devices can communicate effectively thanks to protocols. Some typical network protocols are listed below:

a. **Transmit Control Protocol/Internet Protocol (TCP/IP):** The internet's primary set of protocols is TCP/IP. It offers dependable, connection-oriented communication, guaranteeing error-free data transfer.
b. HTTP is commonly used for web browsing, and SMTP

is frequently used for email. Hypertext Transfer Protocol/ Secure Hypertext Transfer Protocol, or HTTP/HTTPS. Web pages and other types of web material are transmitted using HTTP. Data is encrypted for secure online transactions using HTTPS, a secure variant of HTTP.

c. **File Transfer Protocol (FTP):** File transfers between a client and a server take place via FTP. It enables users to send files to and download them from distant servers.
d. **(SMTP/POP3/IMAP):** Simple Mail Transfer Protocol, Post Office Protocol, and Internet Message Access Protocol. Email messages are sent, received, and accessed using these protocols.
e. **Domain Name System (DNS):** DNS converts domain names that can be read by humans into IP addresses, making it easier to use websites and other internet services.
f. **Secure Shell (SSH):** Data transport and secure remote access are both offered by SSH across encrypted connections. It is frequently employed for controlling distant servers.
g. **Ethernet:** At the data link layer (Layer 2), Ethernet is a widely used LAN protocol. It specifies how devices connected to the same network segment communicate and how data packets are deposited on the physical medium.
h. **Wireless Protocols (such as Bluetooth and Wi-Fi):** These protocols make it possible for wireless LANs, personal area networks, and other types of wireless communication between devices.
i. **Virtual Private Network Protocols:** Public networks can be utilized to establish safe, encrypted connections thanks to VPN technologies like OpenVPN and IPsec.
j. **Voice over Internet Protocol (VoIP):** VoIP protocols, which are frequently used for internet telephony, allow

voice and multimedia communication over IP networks. In order to develop, manage, and debug network infrastructures, network administrators, engineers, and anybody else dealing with computer networks must have a solid understanding of network topologies and protocols. The specific requirements of the network and the applications it serves determine the topology and protocols that should be used.

Chapter 7: Computer Security

The practice of defending computer systems, networks, and data from various dangers, vulnerabilities, and attacks is known as computer security, also referred to as cybersecurity. Computer security is now a top priority for people, companies, and governments in our increasingly linked and digital world. The following are some crucial elements of computer security:

7.1. Threats to Computer Security:

a. **Malware:** Computers can become infected with malicious software, such as viruses, worms, Trojan horses, and ransomware, which can then steal data, interfere with operations, or corrupt files.
b. **Cyberattacks:** Hacking, denial-of-service (DoS), and distributed denial-of-service (DDoS) assaults are a few examples of cyberattacks that try to jeopardize the availability and integrity of networks.
c. **Phishing:** Phishing attacks utilize misleading emails or websites to fool people into disclosing sensitive information, such login passwords or financial information.
d. **Social Engineering:** Attackers who practice social engineering manipulate people's minds to persuade them to divulge sensitive information or take security-compromising behaviours.
e. **Data Breaches:** Sensitive information may be exposed as a result of unauthorized access to databases or systems, posing a risk of identity theft and privacy violations.

7.2. Security Measures

a. **Firewalls:** By observing incoming and outgoing traffic and preventing illegal access, firewalls serve as barriers between a network and possible dangers.

b. **Antivirus Software:** Malicious software is found and eliminated from computers and networks using antivirus and anti-malware software.
c. **Encryption:** Using an unreadable format that can only be decoded by those with the encryption key, encryption technology assures that data is secure.
d. **Access Control**: Passwords, biometrics, and multi-factor authentication (MFA) are examples of access control systems that only allow authorized users access.
e. **Regular Updates**: To address known vulnerabilities, it's essential to keep software, operating systems, and security patches up to date.
f. **Security Policies**: To specify how information and resources should be protected, organizations set up security policies and procedures, and staff are trained to abide by these rules.

7.3. Best Practices for Cybersecurity

a. **Awareness:** Users should be made aware of security threats and safe computing procedures to lessen their vulnerability to online attacks.
b. **Backup**: Consistent data backup ensures that crucial data may be restored in the event of data loss due to a hacker attack or device failure.
c. **Plan for Incident Response**: Organizations should have a plan for responding to and mitigating security issues in place at all times.
d. **Security Audits:** Regular security audits and vulnerability assessments strengthen an organization's security posture by highlighting areas for improvement.

7.4. Considerations of Law and Morality:

a. **Data Protection Laws:** To protect individual privacy and mandate that businesses secure sensitive data, many nations have passed data protection laws and regulations.
b. **Ethical Hacking**: Organizations use ethical hackers, often referred to as penetration testers, to find security flaws in their systems before hostile hackers can take advantage of them.
c. **Digital Ethics:** In the field of computer security, taking into account aspects of digital ethics, such as privacy, data ownership, and responsible technology usage, is becoming more and more crucial.

The field of computer security is dynamic and continually changing as new threats appear and technology develops. To safeguard their digital assets and uphold the privacy, accuracy, and accessibility of data and systems, people and organizations must always be on guard, adapt to new threats, and have strong security procedures in place.

7.1. Threats and Vulnerabilities

Understanding threats and vulnerabilities is essential for providing effective protection for computer systems and networks. They are significant topics in the field of computer security. Let's examine threats and vulnerabilities and their connections to cybersecurity.

7.1.1. Threat

Threats are potential risks or adverse situations that could take advantage of weaknesses and jeopardize the safety of computer systems, networks, and data. Threats can originate from a variety of places and might be deliberate or accidental.

The following list of typical risks includes:

a. **Malware:** Software that is intended to harm computer systems or steal sensitive data, such as viruses, worms, Trojan horses, spyware, adware, and ransomware.
b. **Cyberattacks:** These are purposeful attempts to undermine the security of computer systems or networks by hackers or other online criminals. Hacking, phishing, denial-of-service (DoS) assaults, and other cyberattacks are frequent.
c. **Insider Threats:** Insider threats happen when those who have been granted access to a system or network abuse that access for evil. This can include workers or contractors purposefully harming others or disclosing private information.
d. **Physical Threats:** Physical threats include things like theft, vandalism, or natural disasters like fires or floods that could physically harm equipment or provide illegal access to physical facilities.
e. **Social Engineering:** Attacks using social engineering take advantage of psychological tricks to persuade people to reveal sensitive information or take security-compromising activities.
f. **Data Breach:** When unauthorized parties access sensitive data, a data breach occurs, frequently leading to data theft, data leaking, and privacy violations.
g. **Zero-Day Vulnerabilities:** These are flaws in hardware or software that have not yet been patched and are unknown to the vendor. Attackers are drawn to zero-day vulnerabilities because there are no existing solutions or safeguards against them.

7.1.2. Vulnerabilities

Vulnerabilities are weak points or faults in software, setups, procedures, or computer systems that can be used by adversaries to undermine the security of the system. A key component of cybersecurity is recognizing and fixing vulnerabilities.

The following list of vulnerabilities is typical:

a. **Software Vulnerabilities**: Are coding faults or defects that an attacker could use to their advantage in software programs, operating systems, or firmware. Buffer overflows, code injection, and unsafe authentication procedures are examples of vulnerabilities.
b. **Configuration Vulnerabilities**: Caused by configuration errors can arise in software, hardware, or network settings. Open ports, weak passwords, or unused system services are a few examples of these.
c. **Outdated Software**: Systems can become vulnerable to known exploits if software and operating systems are not kept up to date with security patches.
d. **Weak Encryption**: Data might be vulnerable to eavesdropping and decryption if weak or obsolete encryption techniques and keys are used.
e. **Human Error:** When sensitive information is handled carelessly or accidentally exposed to the public, it might create security risks.
f. **Third-Party Components:** Third-party libraries or components are used by many systems. If any of these parts are vulnerable, the system as a whole could become less secure.
g. **Lack of Security Controls:** Systems may become exposed to attacks if the proper security measures, such as firewalls, intrusion detection systems, or access controls, are not put in place.

7.1.3. Threats and Vulnerabilities in Relationship:

Threats take advantage of weaknesses to commit crimes. The focus of the cybersecurity industry is on locating vulnerabilities, evaluating the risks they present, and putting in place safeguards to reduce those risks and defend against future attackers. Penetration testing, security audits, vulnerability assessments, and the creation of security policies and procedures are all part of this process.

Organizations and individuals must continuously monitor for new threats, discover and fix vulnerabilities, and adopt security controls and best practices to lessen the chance and impact of security incidents in order to manage cybersecurity efficiently.

7.1.4. Lists common Cyber-threats, how they attack computers, and mitigation strategies

Cyber Threat	Attack Type	Mitigation Strategies
Malware	• Delivered through malicious downloads or email attachments. • Exploits vulnerabilities to gain access and execute malicious code. • Spreads through infected files and networks	✓ Use up-to-date antivirus software. ✓ Regularly update operating systems and software. ✓ Educate users on safe browsing habits. ✓ Implement email filtering and scanning solutions
Phishing	• Deceptive emails, messages, or websites impersonating legitimate entities to trick users into revealing sensitive information. • Can lead to identity theft and financial losses	✓ Train employees to recognize phishing attempts. ✓ Use email authentication (SPF, DKIM, DMARC) to verify email senders. ✓ Employ anti-phishing tools and email filtering

Ransomware	• Encrypts files or entire systems and demands a ransom for decryption. • Often delivered via email or exploit kits. • Can spread across networks. • Encrypts files or entire systems and demands a ransom for decryption. • Often delivered via email or exploit kits. • Can spread across networks.	✓ Maintain offline backups of critical data. ✓ Implement robust network security measures. ✓ Train users to avoid suspicious emails and links. ✓ Regularly update and patch software.
DDoS Attacks	• Overwhelm a target system or network with a flood of traffic or requests, causing service disruptions or downtime. • Launched from botnets or multiple compromised devices.	✓ Deploy intrusion detection and prevention systems (IDS/IPS). ✓ Use DDoS mitigation services and content delivery networks (CDNs). ✓ Harden network infrastructure.

		✓ Monitor traffic patterns for anomalies.
Insider Threats	• Threats from employees or trusted individuals with access to sensitive information. • Can be intentional (malicious) or accidental (negligent).	✓ Implement role-based access control (RBAC). ✓ Monitor user activity and behaviour for unusual patterns. ✓ Conduct regular security training and awareness programs. ✓ Enforce the principle of least privilege (PoLP).
Zero-Day Exploits	• Attacks targeting unpatched vulnerabilities that are unknown to software vendors. • Can lead to unauthorized access or data breaches.	✓ Keep systems and software up-to-date with patches. ✓ Employ intrusion detection systems (IDS) and threat intelligence.

		✓ Implement network segmentation to limit lateral movement. ✓ Use application whitelisting.
Social Engineering	• Manipulates individuals into divulging sensitive information or performing actions that compromise security. • Techniques include pretexting, baiting, tailgating, and more.	✓ Train employees to recognize social engineering tactics. ✓ Establish clear security policies and procedures. ✓ Use two-factor authentication (2FA) for access control. ✓ Encourage reporting of suspicious activities.
Man-in-the-Middle (MitM)	• Intercept and potentially modify communication between two parties without their knowledge. • Often targets public Wi-	✓ Use encrypted communication protocols (e.g., HTTPS, VPNs).

	Fi or unencrypted connections.	✓ Verify the authenticity of websites and certificates. ✓ Educate users to avoid unsecured networks and connections.
SQL Injection	• Exploits vulnerabilities in web applications by injecting malicious SQL code. • Allows attackers to manipulate databases and access sensitive data.	✓ Employ secure coding practices and input validation. ✓ Use web application firewalls (WAFs) to filter out malicious input. ✓ Regularly audit and test web applications for vulnerabilities. ✓ Limit database privileges.

Copyright: Patrick Mukosha (2023

Figure 11: Lists common Cyber-threats, how they attack computers, and mitigation strategies

Note: Keep in mind that this is not an exhaustive list of Cyber-threats, and new threats may emerge over time. It's crucial to stay updated on cybersecurity best practices and adapt your mitigation strategies accordingly. Additionally, a comprehensive cybersecurity strategy involves a combination of technical measures, user education, and proactive monitoring.

7.2. Authentication and Authorization

Fundamental ideas in computer security include authentication and authorisation, particularly when it comes to access control and user privileges. Together, these two procedures make sure that users can only access the resources and actions to which they are authorized while safeguarding private information and system integrity. Here is a description of each phrase and how they differ:

7.2.1. Authentication:

Verifying a user, system, or entity's identity when they try to access a computer system, application, or network is the process of authentication. Authentication's main objective is to confirm that the entity claiming a specific identity is, in fact, who it claims to be. Presenting an item that should only belong to a legitimate person or system is often required for authentication:

a. **Username and Passwords:** Authentication using usernames and passwords is the most used type. Users supply a secret password in addition to a username. The system checks the password against its database of saved information.
b. **Biometrics:** Biometric authentication uses a person's distinctive physical or behavioural traits, such as their fingerprints, retinal scans, or facial recognition.
c. **Multi-Factor Authentication (MFA) vs. Two-Factor Authentication (2FA):** To increase security, these techniques integrate two or more authentication factors. For instance, a user could have a mobile device that

generates one-time codes and know their password.

d. **Smart Card or Tokens:** These tangible objects, known as smart cards or tokens, can be used to generate one-time codes or to put into card readers to store authentication credentials.

e. **Certificates:** Digital certificates can be used to confirm the legitimacy of individuals, devices, or websites. These certificates are provided by reputable authorities.

The system or application allows access to the authorized person or entity after the authentication process has been successful.

7.2.2. Authorization:

The process of deciding which activities or resources a verified person or entity is permitted to access or perform within a system is known as authorization, sometimes known as access control. Users can only access resources and features that they are explicitly allowed to use thanks to authorization.

An authorization may include:

a. **Permission Levels:** Users are given particular authorization levels or roles, which dictate their access permissions. A typical user might only have certain access, whereas an administrator might have full access.

b. **Access Control Lists (ACLs)**: Are lists of permissions connected to a certain resource that define who is permitted to carry out particular actions on that resource.

c. **Role-Based Access Control (RBAC):** RBAC assigns roles to users, and each role has a specific set of permissions. Based on their given roles, users inherit certain permissions.

d. **Attribute-Based Access Control (ABAC):** ABAC employs a policy-based approach to access control and weighs a variety of factors, including user attributes, resource attributes, and environmental factors, to decide access.

e. **Contextual Authorisation:** Authorization decisions may also take into account contextual information, such as the user's location, the time of access, and the system's current status.

7.2.3. Differences:

a. While authorization decides which activities or resources the authorized person or entity is permitted to access, authentication confirms the identity of a user or entity.
b. While authorization involves creating and enforcing access rules and permissions, authentication focuses on validating credentials (such as username and password).
c. In the process of access control, authentication usually comes first.
d. Access is controlled through authentication, whereas authorized actions are limited once access has been granted.

Effective access control systems must have both authentication and authorization to make sure that only authorized users may access resources and take activities that are allowed by the organization's rules and security requirements.

7.2.4. The Key differences between Authorization and Authentication

Aspect	Authentication	Authorisation
Definition	Authentication is the process of verifying the identity of a user or system, ensuring that they are who they claim to be.	Authorization is the process of granting or denying access to specific resources or actions based on the authenticated user's permissions or privileges.
Purpose	To establish trust in the identity of a user or system before allowing access to a system or service	To determine what actions or resources an authenticated user is allowed to access or manipulate within a system or application.
Verification	Authentication verifies the user's identity through credentials such as passwords, biometrics, smart cards, or tokens.	Authorization doesn't verify identity but relies on the authenticated identity established through authentication.
Timing	Authentication occurs before authorization.	Authorization occurs after successful authentication.
Focus	Focuses on "Who you are?"	Focuses on "What you are allowed to do or access?"
Examples	• Username and password. • Fingerprint recognition • Two-factor authentication (2FA)	✓ Role-based access control (RBAC) ✓ Access control lists (ACLs) ✓ Permissions and privileges settings
Security Implications	A successful authentication ensures that the user is genuine, preventing unauthorized access.	Authorization ensures that even authenticated users can only access what they are authorized to, minimizing the risk of

		unauthorized actions.
Responsibility	Authentication is typically handled at the login or access point and is often the responsibility of the authentication server.	Authorization is usually controlled within the application or system, defining access rules and permissions.
Common Protocols	• LDAP (Lightweight Directory Access Protocol) for authentication • OAuth for authorization	✓ OAuth (with different scopes) for authorization ✓ Role-based access control (RBAC) mechanisms for authorization
Error Handling	Authentication errors typically include failed logins due to incorrect credentials.	Authorization errors typically involve access denied or insufficient privileges messages.

Copyright: Patrick Mukosha (2023)

Figure 12: The Key differences between Authorization and Authentication

Note: Understanding the distinction between authentication and authorization is essential in designing robust security systems. Authentication ensures that only legitimate users gain access, while authorization defines what actions or resources they can access once authenticated. Both elements are critical components of an effective access control strategy.

7.3. Encryption and Cryptography

In the area of computer security, encryption and cryptography are related concepts that play crucial roles in safeguarding sensitive data and maintaining the confidentiality, integrity, and validity of data.

Let's examine the definitions and principles of encryption and cryptography:

7.3.1. Cryptography: The study and application of secure communication methods that change data into a form that is incomprehensible to unauthorized people is known as cryptography. It involves encoding and decoding data using mathematical procedures and techniques.

Cryptography offers a number of crucial functions:

a. **Confidentiality:** Data confidentiality is aided by cryptography, which hides information from unauthorized parties. The encrypted data can only be read by those who possess the correct decryption key.
b. **Integrity:** Cryptographic methods are capable of identifying any illegal alterations to data. When data is decrypted, any changes made to it during storage or transport become clear.
c. **Authentication:** Using cryptography, it is possible to confirm the parties to a communication or transaction are who they claim to be. A typical cryptographic technique for authentication is the use of digital signatures.
d. **Non-Repudiation:** Cryptographic techniques can make sure that a participant cannot refute their participation in a communication or transaction. For reasons of law and responsibility, this is essential.
e. **Secure Key Exchange:** Cryptography offers strategies for keeping encryption keys private and out of the hands of prying eyes.

7.3.2. Encryption:

A specific use of cryptography is encryption, which converts data from its original, readable form (plaintext) into an unintelligible, encoded form (ciphertext). Algorithms and keys are used in encryption to carry out this transformation.

There are principally two kinds of encryption:

a. **Symmetric Encryption:** The same key is utilized in symmetric encryption for both encryption and decryption. This implies that the same secret key must be held and guarded by both the sender and the recipient. Advanced Encryption Standard (AES) and Data Encryption Standard (DES) are two examples of symmetric encryption methods.
b. **Asymmetric Encryption:** Public-key encryption, also referred to as asymmetric encryption, involves a set of two keys: a public key and a private key. While the private key is required for decryption, the public key is utilized for encryption. While the recipient's private key is kept confidential, their public key is made public. The requirement for key exchange is removed by this strategy. Elliptic Curve Cryptography (ECC) and RSA are two popular asymmetric encryption techniques.

7.3.3. How Cryptography Operates:

Data that has to be encrypted is processed using an encryption algorithm and either the recipient's public key for symmetric encryption or a secret key for asymmetric encryption. As a result, the ciphertext seems to be unorganized data. The ciphertext is transmitted via a network or kept in a safe place.

The recipient can recover the original plaintext by decrypting the ciphertext if they have the necessary decryption key (either the same secret key in the case of symmetric encryption or their private key in the case of asymmetric encryption). The ciphertext is unreadable and unintelligible to anyone who lacks the proper decryption key.

Encryption is frequently used to safeguard data at rest (stored on devices or servers), secure conversations over the internet, and guarantee the secrecy of sensitive data. It is an important part of cybersecurity and is crucial for protecting digital assets and privacy.

7.3.4. Key differences between Encryption and Cryptography

Aspect	Encryption	Cryptography
Definition	Encryption is a specific process within cryptography that involves converting plaintext into ciphertext to secure data.	Cryptography is the broader field that encompasses various techniques and methods for securing communication and information.
Purpose	The primary purpose of encryption is to protect the confidentiality of data by making it unreadable to unauthorized parties.	Cryptography serves a broader purpose, including confidentiality (encryption), integrity verification, authentication, and non-repudiation.
Process	Encryption is one specific process within the field of cryptography, involving algorithms and keys to transform data into a secure form.	Cryptography includes encryption, decryption, digital signatures, key management, and other techniques to achieve its goals.
Focus	Focuses on the transformation of data from plaintext to ciphertext using encryption algorithms and keys.	Encompasses a wider range of cryptographic techniques and concepts, including encryption, decryption, key generation, and more.
Components	Encryption involves encryption algorithms, encryption keys, plaintext, and ciphertext.	Cryptography involves encryption, decryption, digital signatures, hash functions, key exchange protocols, and more.
Security Goal	The primary security goal of encryption is to ensure the confidentiality of data by making it unreadable without the appropriate decryption key.	Cryptography aims to achieve various security goals, including confidentiality, integrity, authenticity, and non-repudiation, depending on the

		context.
Application	Encryption is widely used for securing data at rest (stored data) and data in transit (communications) in various applications.	Cryptography is applied in various fields, including secure communications, digital signatures, secure authentication, and secure key exchange.
Examples	• AES (Advanced Encryption Standard) • RSA encryption • Symmetric and asymmetric encryption methods	✓ Public key infrastructure (PKI) ✓ Digital signatures ✓ Hash functions ✓ Key exchange protocols (e.g., Diffie-Hellman)
Practical Use	Encryption is a practical application of cryptographic principles, focusing on data protection through secure transformation.	Cryptography is the overarching field used to address various security challenges in information systems, communications, and cryptography itself.
Key Management	Encryption often involves key management to securely generate, store, and distribute encryption keys.	Cryptography encompasses key management as part of its broader scope, including key generation, distribution, and protection.
Common Usage Scenarios	Encryption is commonly used in securing sensitive data, such as financial transactions, passwords, and confidential communications.	Cryptography is used in various scenarios, such as securing communications, ensuring the authenticity of digital documents, and protecting data integrity.

Copyright: Patrick Mukosha (2023)

Figure 13: Key differences between Encryption and Cryptography

Note: Encryption is a specific technique within the broader field of cryptography. Encryption focuses on converting plaintext into ciphertext to achieve data confidentiality, while cryptography encompasses a wider range of techniques and goals, including encryption, decryption, digital signatures, key management, and more, to address various security requirements in information systems and communications.

7.4. Firewalls and Intrusion Detection Systems

Network security is not complete without firewalls and intrusion detection systems (IDS), which assist shield computer systems and networks from unwanted access, cyberattacks, and potential security lapses. Each plays a particular function in protecting network resources. Let's examine the definitions, purposes, and differences of firewalls and intrusion detection systems.

7.4.1. Firewalls:

An organization's LAN, for example, and untrusted external networks (usually the internet) are separated by a firewall, a network security device or piece of software. A firewall's main job is to regulate and keep track of network traffic using pre-established security rules and regulations.

Firewalls' essential features include:

a. **Filtering Traffic:** Firewalls examine network traffic and categorize it according to predetermined criteria. These rules may include allowing or blocking traffic based on IP addresses, ports, protocols, or particular application signatures.

b. **Access Control:** Firewalls carry out regulations governing access control, allowing or prohibiting network communication between various network segments or devices.

c. **Stateful Inspection:** To keep track of the status of active connections, modern firewalls employ stateful inspection. They are able to distinguish between incoming requests that are legitimately answered and traffic that might be fraudulent.

d. **Network Address Translation (NAT):** NAT technology

is found in many firewalls, and it allows for the concealment of internal IP addresses from outside networks, hence boosting security and privacy.

e. **Application Layer Filtering:** Some cutting-edge firewalls are able to inspect traffic at the application layer (Layer 7) and make choices depending on particular services or apps, giving granular control.
f. **Proxy Services:** In order to offer an extra degree of protection, firewalls can function as proxies, intercepting and examining communication before sending it to its destination.

7.4.2. Intrusion Detecting Systems (IDS):

A security tool known as an intrusion detection system (IDS) watches over network or system activity for indications of malicious or unauthorized activity or policy violations. IDS is intended to identify and notify on suspicious activity, as opposed to firewalls, which concentrate on traffic control.

IDS's main features include:

a. **Anomaly Detection:** IDS systems are capable of detecting anomalies—differences from typical network or system behaviour. To do this, baselines of expected behaviour are established, and warnings are sent when abnormalities arise.
b. **Signature-Based Detection:** Some IDS employ signature-based detection, which is a feature of antivirus software, to identify well-known malware, exploits, and attack patterns.
c. **Alerts and Notifications:** IDS generates alerts and notifications to network administrators or security workers when suspicious behaviour is discovered. Information about the observed occurrence may be included in these warnings.
d. **Passive and Active Modes:** IDS can be used in either a

passive or active mode of operation. While active IDS can block traffic in reaction to threats it detects, passive IDS can just monitor and alarm.

e. **Host-Based and Network-Based IDS:** Host-Based IDS (HIDS) concentrates on monitoring specific servers or devices, whereas Network-Based IDS (NIDS) examines network traffic.
f. **Behaviour Analysis:** Advanced IDS systems use behavioural analysis approaches to identify threats that may lack well-known signatures by observing deviations from expected behaviour.

7.4.3. Differences:

a. **Function:** While IDS monitors network and system activities to look for indications of suspect or illegal behaviour, firewalls primarily manage and filter network traffic based on established rules.
b. **Action:** When suspicious activity is discovered, IDS provide warnings and notifications, while firewalls decide whether to allow or stop traffic.
c. **Focus:** IDS focuses on identifying security incidents and threats, while firewalls concentrate on blocking unauthorized access and filtering traffic.
d. **Deployment:** Firewalls are normally installed at network borders, whereas IDS can be installed inside networks or on specific servers.

In reality, enterprises frequently employ IDS in addition to firewalls as a complimentary security solution. As access control policies are enforced and the network perimeter is protected by firewalls, intrusion detection systems (IDS) offer more visibility into potential threats and can help with security incident response. They strengthen network security as a whole and aid enterprises in maintaining a robust security posture.

7.4.4. Key Differences between Firewalls and Intrusion Detection Systems (IDS)

Aspect	Firewalls	Intrusion Detection Systems (IDS)
Definition	**Firewalls** are network security devices that control incoming and outgoing network traffic based on predefined security rules and policies	**IDS** are security systems designed to detect and alert on suspicious or malicious activities within a network or system.
Function	Firewalls act as a barrier between a trusted internal network and untrusted external networks, filtering traffic based on set rules to permit or deny access.	IDS passively monitor network traffic or system events, analyzing patterns to identify potential security breaches or anomalies.
Action on Detection	Firewalls primarily block or allow traffic based on predefined rules, providing an active barrier against unwanted access.	IDS focus on alerting administrators or security personnel about suspicious activities; they don't block traffic but aid in detection and response.
Focus	Firewalls are mainly focused on traffic control and access management, often at the network or transport layer of the OSI model.	IDS focus on analyzing content and behavior at higher layers (e.g., application layer) to detect intrusion attempts or anomalies.
Deployment Location	Typically, firewalls are deployed at network boundaries, such as between an internal network and the internet, to filter incoming and outgoing traffic.	IDS sensors can be distributed throughout a network, monitoring traffic and events at multiple points, including within the internal network.
Traffic Handling	Firewalls examine traffic based on predefined criteria, such as source IP, destination IP, ports,	IDS analyze traffic or events for patterns or signatures that match known attack patterns,

	and protocols, and enforce access policies accordingly	generating alerts when detected.
Blocking Capabilities	Firewalls have the ability to block or permit traffic in real-time, actively preventing unauthorized access based on defined rules	IDS do not block traffic; they notify administrators or security teams about suspicious activities, allowing for manual intervention.
False Positives	Firewalls tend to generate fewer false positives because they follow strict rule-based filtering and blocking.	IDS may generate more false positives because they focus on detecting anomalies or matching patterns, which can lead to alerts for non-malicious activities
Types	Types of firewalls include network firewalls, stateful inspection firewalls, application layer firewalls (proxy), and more.	Types of IDS include network-based IDS (NIDS) and host-based IDS (HIDS), each serving different purposes in monitoring.
Use in Security Strategy	Firewalls are a fundamental component of network security, serving as a first line of defense against unauthorized access.	IDS complement other security measures by providing insight into potential threats and helping with incident response and forensics.
Examples	• Cisco ASA • Palo Alto Networks Firewall • iptables (Linux-based firewall)	✓ Snort (NIDS) ✓ Suricata (NIDS) ✓ OSSEC (HIDS)

Copyright: Patrick Mukosha (2023)

Figure 14: Key Differences between Firewalls and Intrusion Detection Systems (IDS)

Note: Firewalls are proactive security devices that control traffic based on predefined rules, actively blocking or permitting network traffic. IDS, on the other hand, are passive monitoring systems that detect and alert on suspicious activities or anomalies within a network, aiding in threat detection and incident response. Both firewalls and IDS play crucial roles in a comprehensive security strategy, with firewalls primarily focused on access control and IDS focused on intrusion detection and alerting.

7.5. Cybersecurity Best Practices

Best practices for cybersecurity are fundamental principles and procedures that people and organizations should adhere to in order to safeguard their computer networks, systems, data, and sensitive information against online threats and attacks. By putting these procedures in place, the danger of security and data breaches is decreased.

Here are some essential best practices for cybersecurity:

7.5.1. Maintain Current Software and Systems: Update firmware, software programs, and operating systems frequently to fix known vulnerabilities. When possible, enable automatic updates to make sure you get urgent security updates.

7.5.2. **Use Secure, Special Passwords:** Make complicated, powerful passwords by combining numbers, letters, special characters, and upper- and lowercase letters. Useless information like birthdays or frequent nouns should be avoided. Create a different password for each system or account. To create and securely store complicated passwords, think about utilizing a reliable password manager.

7.5.2. **Use MFA (multi-factor authentication):** Wherever possible, enable MFA to offer an additional degree of security. Typically, this requires both something you have (such a mobile device that generates a one-time code) and something you know (a password).

7.5.4. **Consistently Backup Your Data**: Important data should be regularly backed up, and backups should be securely stored. To guarantee that data can be properly restored in the event of data loss or ransomware attacks, test backups.

7.5.5. **Train and Educate Employees:** To help all employees spot phishing efforts, social engineering, and other security dangers, conduct cybersecurity awareness training for them. Encourage the organization to adopt a security-conscious culture and ethical computing practices.

7.5.6. **Use Antivirus and Malware Protection Software**: All equipment, including servers, workstations, and mobile devices, should have reliable antivirus and anti-malware software installed and updated on a regular basis.

7.5.7. **Manage Privileges and Access**: Use the principle of least privilege (PoLP) to limit users' access to systems to only what is essential for them to do their jobs. Restrict privileges that are not necessary on a regular basis.

7.5.8. **Secure Sensitive Information:** Protect sensitive data with encryption, both during transmission (e.g., utilizing HTTPS) and storage (e.g., whole disk encryption).

7.5.9. **Keep track of network traffic**: Monitor network traffic for unusual or suspicious activities by implementing intrusion detection and prevention systems (IDS/IPS) and security information and event management (SIEM) solutions.

7.5.10. **Create a Documented Incident Response strategy**: This strategy should specify how to handle security incidents, such as data breaches and cyberattacks. To make sure the strategy remains effective, test and revise it frequently.

7.5.11. **Secure Physical Access:** Use physical security measures including locks, security badges, and surveillance cameras. Restrict physical access to server rooms and essential infrastructure components.

7.5.12. **Regularly Conduct Security Audits and Assessments:** Periodically evaluate and audit the security posture of your organization, including penetration testing and vulnerability assessments.

7.5.13. **Implement Vendor Security:** Evaluate the security procedures used by outside vendors and service providers who have access to the data or systems of your firm.

7.5.14. **Create and Communicate Clear Security Policies and Procedures**, and apply them consistently throughout the organization.

7.5.15. **Keep Up-To-Date With Emerging Risks**: Keep track of business news, threat intelligence feeds, and security advisories to stay informed about the most recent cybersecurity risks and trends.

7.5.16. **Segment Your Network:** Limit the lateral movement of attackers inside your network by segmenting it into distinct zones or VLANs.

Cybersecurity is a continual process that calls for ongoing attention to detail and response to changing threats. Individuals and organizations may greatly enhance their cybersecurity posture and lower the risk of cyber events by adhering to these best practices and promoting a culture of security.

Chapter 8: System Performance and Optimisation

8.1. Introduction:

Critical components of managing computer systems and networks are system performance and optimization. For both enterprises and individuals, ensuring that systems operate effectively, dependably, and to their maximum capacity is crucial. We'll look at many facets of system performance, optimization methods, and recommended practices in this chapter.

1. **Learning about System Performance:**

- Establish performance indicators for the system, such as CPU and memory usage, disk I/O, and network throughput.
- Utilize resources like Task Manager, Resource Monitor, and performance monitoring software to measure and keep an eye on system performance.
- Recognize how resource limitations and system bottlenecks affect performance.

1. **Finding Performance Bottlenecks**

- Identify the typical performance bottlenecks, such as network, CPU, RAM, disk I/O, and memory bottlenecks.
- To identify the underlying causes of performance, use performance monitoring tools.

1. **Strategies for System Optimization:**

- Investigate optimization methods to boost system

efficiency and resource use.

- To improve system responsiveness, optimize the usage of CPU, memory, storage, and network resources.
- Use best practices to cut down on unneeded background operations and system overhead.

1. **Storage and Disk Optimization:**

- By defragmenting disks, utilizing SSDs, and designing effective file systems, you may increase disk and storage performance.
- To decrease access times and enhance data retrieval, become familiar with storage tiering and caching.

1. **Optimisation of the Network:**

- Utilize methods to improve network performance, such as load balancing, Quality of Service (QoS) configurations, and network protocol optimization.
- To manage and optimize network traffic, use traffic shaping and network monitoring.

1. **Memory Control:**

- Recognize virtual memory, paging, and swapping principles in memory management.
- Use memory-saving strategies like memory compression and modifying virtual memory settings.

1. **Optimization of the CPU:**

- Utilize methods like parallel processing, multi-threading, and process priority to increase CPU performance.

- Find out about CPU affinity and how it works to assign CPU resources to particular workloads.

1. **System Configuration and Tuning:**

- Investigate the configuration options and system tuning parameters in operating systems and apps.
- Configure the system settings to match certain performance and resource needs.

1. **Performance Analysis and Monitoring Tools:**

- Learn about tools for monitoring and analysing performance, such as PerfMon for Windows, top for Linux/Unix, and third-party performance analysis programs.
- Utilize these tools to gather performance information, examine patterns, and resolve performance problems.

1. **Cloud optimization and virtualization:**

- Learn about performance-enhancing virtualized environments (like VMware and Hyper-V) and cloud-based resources.
- Recognize how load balancing, scalability, and resource allocation operate in virtual and cloud settings.

1. **Resolving Performance Problems**

- Develop your troubleshooting abilities to identify and fix issues with system performance.
- Use a methodical process to identify and address performance issues.

1. **Recommended Techniques for System Optimization**

- Implement recommended practices for system performance maintenance, such as routine updates, backups, and system upkeep.
- To aid in troubleshooting and optimization, document system setups and modifications.
- Balance between security and performance:
- Think about how system performance and security measures interact.
- Implement security measures that secure data while having a minimal impact on system performance.

You will be better able to manage, optimize, and troubleshoot system performance if you grasp the concepts and methods covered in this chapter. These abilities will aid you in maintaining the dependability and effectiveness of your computing environment, regardless of whether you are in charge of simple networked systems or numerous individual computers.

8.2. Performance Metrics and Benchmarks

For assessing and analysing the performance of computer systems, hardware, software, and networks, performance metrics and benchmarks are crucial tools. In order to evaluate how well a system or component is operating and whether it satisfies particular needs or expectations, they offer objective data and comparisons. Let's delve deeper into performance measurements and benchmarks:

8.2.1. Performance Measurements

Performance metrics are numerical measurements that are employed to evaluate different facets of system performance. Depending on the situation and the particular system or component being assessed, these measurements may change.

Here are a few typical performance indicators:

a. **Response Time:** Response time gauges how quickly a program or system reacts to user input or requests. It is crucial for user experience, especially in interactive applications, and is frequently stated in milliseconds (ms).
b. **Throughput:** The rate at which a system or component can process or handle data or requests is known as throughput. It is frequently represented in terms of data transfer rates (such as Mbps for networks) or transactions per second (TPS).
c. **Latency:** The *time elapsed between sending a request and getting a response* is known as *latency*. In real-time applications like online gaming and financial trading, low-latency systems are essential.
d. **Resource Usage:** Metrics for resource usage include CPU and memory usage, disk I/O rates, and network bandwidth consumption. High resource use may be a sign of

performance problems or bottlenecks.

e. **Error Rates**: are a way of measuring how frequently a system makes mistakes or fails. This may involve lost network packets, hardware malfunctions, or software issues.
f. **Scalability:** Scalability metrics evaluate a system's capacity to accommodate growing user demand or workload. Systems that must handle growth must be scalable.
g. **Uptime and availability metrics** calculate the proportion of time a system is available to users and operating. Uptime, which is measured as a percentage, is the opposite of downtime.
h. **Power Efficiency:** Metrics for power efficiency assess the energy use of hardware parts or data centres. Green computing techniques strive to keep performance high while consuming less electricity.
i. **Quality of Service (QoS) measures**, frequently expressed in terms of packet loss, jitter, and delay, are used to assess the level of service offered by networks or communication systems.

8.2.2. Benchmarks:

The performance of certain hardware, software, or systems is measured through benchmarks, which are standardized tests or sets of tasks. They offer a reliable technique to contrast various items or setups. Benchmarks frequently used include:

a. **CPU Benchmarks**: These tests use a variety of computing workloads to measure a CPU's processing power. Examples include the PassMark CPU benchmark and the SPEC CPU benchmark package.
b. **Graphics Benchmarks:** Graphics benchmarks rate the efficiency of graphics cards and GPUs (Graphics Processing Units). A couple of well-known graphics tests include

3DMark and Unigine Heaven.

c. **Disk and Storage Benchmarks:** Hard drives (HDDs) and solid-state drives (SSDs) are among the storage devices whose read and write speeds are measured by disk benchmarks. Examples include CrystalDiskMark and ATTO Disk Benchmark.
d. **Network Benchmarks:** Network benchmarks evaluate the functionality of network interfaces, switches, and routers. Network benchmarking is done with the help of programs like iPerf and NetBench.
e. **Database Benchmarks:** By carrying out numerous database activities, database benchmarks assess the effectiveness of database management systems (DBMS). Frequently used database benchmarks include TPC-C and TPC-H.
f. **Web Server Benchmarks** measure how well web servers operate under various traffic and load conditions. Examples include Siege and ApacheBench.
g. **Operating System Benchmarks:** Using a variety of system-level tasks, these benchmarks assess the performance of operating systems. A flexible tool for OS benchmarking is the Phoronix Test Suite.
h. **Benchmarks for Mobile Devices**: Benchmarks for mobile devices assess the CPU, GPU, and battery life of smartphones and tablets. Mobile benchmarking uses Geekbench and AnTuTu.

8.2.3. Why Benchmarks and Performance Metrics Matter:

a. **Comparison:** They make it possible to compare various systems, parts, or configurations fairly and impartially.
b. **Baseline:** Benchmarks can create performance baselines for systems, which can be used to spot errors or potential

improvements.

c. **Tuning:** Metrics and benchmarks help with system optimization to ensure optimum performance.
d. **Validation:** They assist in validating if a system complies with service level agreements (SLAs) or performance standards.
e. **Troubleshooting**: Metrics aid in diagnosing and locating performance bottlenecks and problems during troubleshooting.

Choosing benchmark tests that are pertinent to your unique use case and workload is crucial when utilizing benchmarks. Consider real-world settings and workloads as well, as synthetic benchmarks might not be accurate.

8.3. Bottlenecks and Optimization Strategies

Computer system bottlenecks are areas of congestion or performance restrictions where resources are unable to keep up with the demands placed on them. For enhancing system performance and guaranteeing effective resource use, bottlenecks must be located and optimization techniques must be put into practice.

The following list of typical bottlenecks and optimization techniques:

8.3.1. Processor Bottlenecks:

- **CPU Bottleneck:** When processing tasks like running apps, calculations, or server requests, the CPU (central processing unit) becomes the limiting element.

Optimization Techniques

- Utilize parallel processing and multi-threading to split up jobs among several CPU cores.
- CPU Affinity: To improve resource allocation, assign particular processes or threads to specific CPU cores.
- Reduce CPU-intensive activities by optimizing software code and methods.
- Offload duties: Use specialized hardware or threads to carry out non-CPU duties, such as I/O operations.

8.3.2. Memory Bottlenecks (RAM):

- Memory Bottlenecks: Slow performance is caused when a system's RAM (Random Access Memory) is unable to handle the simultaneous load of data and operations.

Optimization Techniques

- RAM upgrade: Increase the system's memory to support heavier workloads.
- Review and improve memory-intensive processes or programs to optimize memory usage.
- Employ caching techniques to keep frequently accessed material in memory for quicker retrieval.
- Monitor Memory Usage: Keep track of how much memory is being used and look for memory leaks or inefficient resource use.

8.3.3. Bottlenecks in disk I/O:

- **Disk I/O bottlenecks** happen when the performance of read and write operations on storage devices (such HDDs or SSDs) becomes constrained, resulting in sluggish data access.

Optimization Techniques

- Upgrade your storage by switching from HDDs to SSDs, which offer noticeably quicker I/O performance.
- RAID setups: For better data redundancy and I/O performance, use RAID (Redundant Array of Independent Disks) setups.
- To distribute the I/O load, organize data into partitions or volumes.
- Choose effective file systems and set them up for greater I/O performance through optimizing file systems.

8.3.4. Bottlenecks in the Network:

When the network infrastructure, such as routers, switches, or network interfaces, is unable to accommodate the level of traffic, bottlenecks in the network might develop.

Optimization Techniques

- Increase network bandwidth or think about employing 10 GbE or fiber optic connections as alternatives.
- Distribute network traffic uniformly over several network links or pathways by using load balancing.
- Prioritize network traffic according to Quality of Service (QoS) standards to make sure that key applications get enough bandwidth.
- Network Monitoring: To locate areas of congestion and improve network settings, use network monitoring tools.

8.3.5. Bottlenecks in Databases:

Database bottlenecks: Slow query execution and data retrieval result from the database server's performance reaching a limit.

Optimization Techniques

- Indexing: To hasten the execution of queries, properly index database tables.
- Optimize database queries by lowering the number of joins and sub questions and by adopting effective database design.
- Implement caching techniques in databases to keep frequently accessed data in memory.
- Database scaling: To accommodate higher workloads, take into account horizontal or vertical database scaling.

8.3.6. Bottlenecks at the Application Level:

Application-level bottlenecks can be brought on by inefficient software code, memory leaks, or subpar application algorithms.

Optimization Techniques

- Code profiling: To locate performance bottlenecks in application code, use profiling tools.
- Refactor code to increase effectiveness, decrease resource use, and speed up execution.
- Memory management: Fix memory leaks and optimize how the application uses its memory.
- Algorithm Optimization: Pick and use effective algorithms for computation and data processing.

8.3.7. Bottlenecks on Web Servers:

Web server bottlenecks can happen when a web server is unable to effectively handle incoming HTTP requests, resulting in sluggish response times.

Optimization Techniques

- Load balancing should be used to split up web traffic among several servers.
- Caching: To reduce the strain on web servers, use caching technologies to store and provide static material.
- Use content delivery networks (CDNs) to serve content from geographically dispersed servers that is closer to the end user.
- Optimize web server configuration options such connection caps and thread pools.

A solid understanding of the system architecture and performance monitoring tools is necessary for locating and resolving bottlenecks. Regular performance improvement and analysis efforts can ensure that computer systems function effectively and satisfy user requests.

8.3.8. Key differences between System Performance and System Optimization

Aspect	System Performance	System Optimisation
Definition	**System Performance** refers to how efficiently a computer or system is currently operating, often measured by metrics like speed, responsiveness, and resource utilization.	**System Optimization** involves improving the efficiency and effectiveness of a computer or system by making adjustments to enhance its overall performance.
Focus	Performance analysis focuses on monitoring and evaluating the current state of the system to identify bottlenecks, slowdowns, or resource constraints.	Optimization focuses on making changes and adjustments to the system to enhance its performance, often targeting specific areas of improvement.
Measurement	Performance is measured using metrics like CPU usage, memory usage, disk I/O, network latency, response times, and throughput.	Optimization progress is evaluated by measuring improvements in the same performance metrics or through benchmarks.
Goal	The goal of performance analysis is to understand how well or poorly a system is performing and identify areas that need improvement.	The goal of system optimization is to actively improve the system's performance, often by reducing resource usage, enhancing responsiveness, or achieving specific performance targets.
Timing	Performance analysis is an ongoing process that provides insights into the current state of the system at a given point in time.	Optimization is a proactive or reactive process where changes are made to improve performance based on analysis and identified areas for improvement.
Activities	Performance monitoring, profiling, and troubleshooting	Optimization activities may include hardware upgrades,

	are common activities in performance analysis.	software tuning, code optimization, caching strategies, and resource allocation adjustments.
Tools and Techniques	Performance analysis relies on tools like monitoring software, profiling tools, and log analysis to gather and analyze performance data.	System optimization uses various techniques such as code refactoring, database indexing, load balancing, and hardware upgrades to enhance performance.
Impact on Resources	Performance analysis typically does not directly impact system resources but helps in identifying resource bottlenecks.	System optimization often involves making changes that can impact resource utilization, such as reducing CPU or memory usage.
Performance Tuning	Performance tuning may involve short-term adjustments to alleviate immediate issues but doesn't always focus on long-term optimization.	System optimization aims to achieve sustained improvements in performance over the long term.
Examples	• Monitoring CPU usage to identify spikes. • Profiling software to find performance bottlenecks. • Analyzing logs for performance-related errors.	✓ Upgrading hardware components like adding more RAM. ✓ Implementing a content delivery network (CDN) for faster web page loading. ✓ Optimizing database queries for efficiency.

Figure 15: Key differences between System Performance and System Optimization

Note: System performance analysis focuses on assessing the current state of a system, while system optimization involves actively making changes to enhance performance based on identified areas for improvement. Both are essential aspects of managing and maintaining efficient computer systems and applications

8.4. Load Balancing and Scalability

In developing and operating computer systems and networks, particularly in settings with heavy traffic or fluctuating workloads, load balancing and scalability are essential concepts. They guarantee that resources are used effectively and that systems can cope with rising demand. Let's look at load balancing, scalability, and how these things relate:

8.4.1. Load Balancing

In order to maintain optimal resource use, maximize performance, and prevent overload on any single resource, load balancing is the process of dividing network traffic or workloads across various resources, such as servers.

These are the main objectives of load balancing:

a. **Effective Resource Utilization**: By evenly distributing traffic or workloads among resources, one can avoid under- or overusing particular servers and cut down on resource waste.
b. **High Availability**: Load balancers may identify failing or unhealthy resources and divert traffic away from them, ensuring continuous service availability.
c. **Increased Performance:** By distributing the load, users have quicker service access and shorter response times.
d. **Scalability:** Load balancers make it possible to add new resources to meet growing demand without interfering with service.

Typical load balancing strategies and procedures include:

a. **Round Robin:** Each server receives requests in turn, consecutively.

b. The server with the fewest active connections will receive traffic.
c. **Weighted Round Robin**: Servers are given weights based on their capacity to distribute traffic inequitably.
d. **IP Hash:** To ensure session persistence, traffic is routed to a server based on the source or destination IP address.
e. **Content-Based Routing**: When choosing a routing path, load balancers take certain content or URL paths into account.
f. **Session Affinity (Sticky Sessions):** To preserve session data, requests from the same client are sent to the same server.

Load balancers are frequently used in connection with server farms or clusters and can be either hardware appliances or software-based solutions. They are frequently used to increase performance and reliability in web applications, database servers, and other distributed systems:

8.4.2. Scalability:

A system's capacity to manage expanding workloads and demand while preserving or enhancing performance without significantly altering its architecture is known as scalability. Scalability seeks to support more users, data, or transactions without degrading service or creating bottlenecks in the system.

The two main categories of scalability are:

a. **Vertical Scalability (Scaling Up):** Resources on a single server or instance are raised to withstand heavier loads in vertical scalability (scaling up). This could entail upgrading the hardware to include extra CPU cores, RAM, or storage space.
b. **Horizontal Scalability (Also Known As Scaling Out)**: In order to improve the capacity of a distributed system,

horizontal scalability (also known as scaling out) entails adding more instances or nodes. To do this, more servers or virtual machines that can each handle a fraction of the burden are deployed.

Scalability-related key ideas include the following:

a. **Stateless Architectures**: By not storing session-specific data on the server, stateless applications can extend horizontally by adding additional instances.
b. **Database Sharding**: To spread the workload across several servers, sharding entails breaking a huge database into smaller, independent pieces (shards).
c. **Cloud Scalability:** refers to the ability of cloud computing systems like AWS, Azure, and Google Cloud to dynamically scale resources in response to demand.
d. **Microservices:** By breaking down large monolithic applications into smaller, independent components, the overall scalability of the system is improved.

Scalability and load balancing are related since load balancing is a method frequently employed to achieve it. Load balancers divide incoming traffic among several servers or resources as a system's load rises, enabling the system to handle the increased burden without suffering performance deterioration. Load balancing and horizontal scalability work together to create highly available, high-performance systems that can change course to meet shifting demands.

8.4.3. Key differences between Load Balancing and Scalability

Aspect	Load Balancing	Scalability
Definition	**Load Balancing** is the process of distributing incoming network traffic or workloads across multiple servers or resources to ensure efficient utilization and prevent overload on any one resource.	**Scalability** is the ability of a system, application, or infrastructure to handle increased load by adding resources or scaling vertically or horizontally.
Focus	Load balancing primarily deals with optimizing resource utilization, maintaining availability, and ensuring even distribution of incoming requests.	Scalability focuses on the ability of a system to grow or expand its capacity to handle higher workloads or users.
Purpose	The primary purpose of load balancing is to improve the performance, availability, and fault tolerance of a system by distributing traffic effectively	Scalability aims to address the long-term capacity needs of a system, ensuring it can accommodate growth without compromising performance.
Mechanism	Load balancing uses various algorithms (e.g., round-robin, least-connections) to distribute incoming requests to available resources.	Scalability involves adding or removing resources (vertical scaling) or replicating components (horizontal scaling) to meet demand.
Use Cases	Load balancing is often used in web servers, application servers, database clusters, and content delivery networks (CDNs) to evenly distribute traffic.	Scalability is relevant in scenarios where a system must handle increased users, data, or processing demands, such as e-commerce websites, cloud services, and social media platforms.

Immediate Impact	Load balancing provides immediate benefits by optimizing resource usage, enhancing availability, and preventing overloads.	Scalability may require planning and implementation, making it a longer-term strategy to accommodate growth.
Hardware vs. Software	Load balancing can be implemented using hardware appliances or software-based load balancers, depending on the requirements and budget.	Scalability can be achieved through both hardware upgrades and software enhancements, as well as cloud-based solutions.
Example Technologies	• Hardware load balancers like F5 BIG-IP. • Software load balancers like Nginx, HAProxy. • Cloud-based load balancing services like AWS ELB.	• Adding more CPU, RAM, or storage to a server (vertical scaling). • Cloning virtual machines or containers (horizontal scaling). • Utilizing auto-scaling groups in cloud environments.
Redundancy	Load balancing often involves redundant load balancers for high availability, but it primarily focuses on distributing traffic.	Scalability considerations include redundancy and fault tolerance, but the primary goal is accommodating growth.
Cost Considerations	Load balancing solutions may require an upfront investment in	Scalability costs may vary depending on the approach,

	hardware or software licenses, but the cost is often justified by improved performance and availability.	such as upgrading hardware, licensing new software instances, or utilizing cloud resources.

Figure 16: Key differences between Load Balancing and Scalability

Note: Load balancing and scalability are related but distinct concepts. Load balancing focuses on optimizing resource utilization and traffic distribution in real-time, while scalability focuses on planning for and accommodating long-term growth in a system's capacity and performance. Both are critical for ensuring the reliability and performance of modern IT systems.

8.5. Caching and Data Access Optimization

In order to increase system performance, decrease latency, and increase the effectiveness of data retrieval, caching and data access optimization are essential strategies. These methods are especially useful when it requires a lot of time or resources to obtain data from the source (such as databases or remote servers). To learn more about caching and data access optimization, read on:

8.5.1. Caching:

Caching is the process of temporarily storing frequently accessed material in a cache so that it can be quickly retrieved later.

These are caching's main goals:

a. **Performance Improvement:** By providing data from a cache, systems can drastically cut response times and operations that use a lot of resources, including network or database calls.
b. **Reduction in Resource Utilisation:** Resource utilization is reduced because to caching, which eases the strain on underlying resources like web servers and databases.
c. **Enhanced Scalability**: By relieving the stress on the original data sources and enabling them to accommodate more concurrent queries, caching can aid in scaling systems.
d. **Improved User Experience:** Faster data access improves the user experience, especially in web applications where page load speeds are crucial.

Typical caching techniques include:

a. **Material Caching:** is the practice of saving frequently used web material (such as HTML, CSS, and images) in a cache to speed up page loads for visitors. Caching like this is frequently used by content delivery networks (CDNs).

b. **Data Caching:** The practice of saving frequently used data, such as API replies or the results of database queries, in order to avoid making repeated network or database requests.
c. **Object Caching:** The practice of storing specific objects or data structures, such as key-value pairs, in memory to speed up application access.
d. **Full-Page Caching**: Storing complete web pages in a cache so that they can be sent rapidly without having to be rendered or processed again.
e. **Browser Caching**: Telling web browsers to keep track of specific assets (such images or scripts) locally on the user's computer to speed up loading for regular users.
f. **Database Query Caching:** Caching database query results allows you to avoid repeating running resource-intensive queries.

8.5.2. Data Access Improvement:

Making data retrieval processes more effective, whether from databases, storage systems, or distant APIs, is the main goal of data access optimization.

Data access optimization's main objectives are:

a. **Reduced Latency:** Reducing the amount of time it takes to retrieve data by streamlining network or query execution.
b. **Minimized Resource Utilization**: To ensure effective resource allocation, lessen the strain on databases, storage systems, and network infrastructure.
c. **Enhanced Query Performance:** Database queries are optimized to retrieve only the information that is required and prevent extraneous processing.

d. **Consistency and Reliability:** Data consistency and dependability are ensured during retrieval, particularly in distributed or multi-tiered systems.

Optimization techniques for data access include:

a. **Database Indexing**: Create and maintain appropriate database indexes to hasten query execution through database indexing.
b. **Query Optimisation**: Reviewing and improving database queries, including query rewriting, the use of joins and indexes, is known as query optimization.
c. **Data Caching**: As previously indicated, data caching helps reduce the need for repetitive data access.
d. **Data Compression:** Using compression techniques to reduce the size of data being transferred or stored in order to increase network and storage efficiency.
e. **Batch Processing**: Multiple data access requests can be combined into batch operations, which can be more effective, especially for network-based access.
f. **Data Sharding and Partitioning** involves breaking up big datasets into smaller, more manageable chunks and dividing the strain of data access among many resources.
g. Distributing data access requests among several servers or nodes to prevent overtaxing certain resources.
h. Using content delivery networks (CDNs) to cache and serve content, such photos and video files, closer to end users would reduce latency.

Effective data access optimization and caching solutions can greatly improve the responsiveness and performance of applications and systems, resulting in better user experiences, cost savings, and more efficient resource use. When adopting caching solutions, it's crucial to take trade-offs into account, such as cache expiration policies and data consistency. Additionally, regular inspection and upkeep are essential to guarantee that cached data is reliable and current.

8.5.3. Key differences between Caching and Data Access Optimization

Aspect	Caching	Data Access Optimisation
Definition	Caching involves storing and retrieving frequently used data or computed results in a faster-accessible location (cache) to improve access times and reduce the load on the primary data source.	Data access optimization refers to strategies and techniques aimed at improving the efficiency of data retrieval and manipulation operations from a data source.
Purpose	The primary purpose of caching is to reduce latency and improve system responsiveness by serving frequently accessed data quickly from a cache rather than fetching it from the original data source.	Data access optimization aims to enhance the overall performance of data retrieval, update, and manipulation processes by optimizing queries, indexing, and data storage structures.
Use Cases	Caching is commonly used in web applications, databases, content delivery networks (CDNs), and file systems to speed up access to frequently used data or content.	Data access optimization is relevant in various scenarios, including database management, search engines, data warehouses, and data-intensive applications.
Mechanism	Caching relies on storing copies of data or computed results in a cache, typically organized in key-value pairs or other data structures, to accelerate access.	Data access optimization involves techniques such as query optimization, indexing, denormalization, and data partitioning to enhance data retrieval and manipulation processes.
Cache Invalidation	Caches need mechanisms to ensure that cached data remains up-to-date; this may involve cache	Data access optimization primarily focuses on optimizing data access patterns but does

	expiration, cache invalidation, or refresh strategies.	not deal with cache management or invalidation.
Freshness vs. Performance	Caches prioritize performance by serving data quickly, potentially sacrificing freshness if not kept up-to-date through cache management strategies.	Data access optimization aims to strike a balance between performance and data freshness by optimizing query execution and data retrieval methods.
Data Consistency	Caching can introduce data consistency challenges, as cached data may not always reflect the latest updates in the primary data source.	Data access optimization focuses on maintaining data consistency while optimizing access methods and query execution.
Storage Type	Caches can be implemented in various ways, such as in-memory caches, disk-based caches, distributed caches, and content delivery networks (CDNs).	Data access optimization primarily involves optimizing the storage and retrieval mechanisms of the primary data source, which can be databases, data lakes, or other data repositories.
Impact on Data Source	Caching reduces the load on the primary data source and can significantly reduce the need for direct queries to the source.	Data access optimization seeks to optimize data source operations directly and may still require some level of direct access to the source.
Real-Time vs. Preprocessing	Caching often involves real-time or on-demand caching, serving cached data as needed.	Data access optimization may involve preprocessing and optimizing data structures or queries in advance to improve performance during retrieval.

Examples	• Browser caching of web page assets. • Database query result caching. • Content delivery network (CDN) caching. • Memoization in programming.	✓ Database indexing for faster query execution. ✓ Query optimization in database management systems. ✓ Data partitioning strategies for data warehouses. ✓ Denormalization to reduce joins and improve read performance.

Copyright: Patrick Mukosha (2023)

Figure 17: Key differences between Caching and Data Access Optimization

Note: Caching focuses on storing frequently accessed data to improve response times, while data access optimization involves various strategies and techniques to optimize data retrieval and manipulation operations directly at the data source. Both approaches are essential for improving system performance and efficiency in different contexts.

Chapter 9: Embedded Systems and IoT

9.1. Introduction:

The Internet of Things (IoT) and embedded systems are two closely related technological fields that are revolutionizing a wide range of industries, from consumer electronics to healthcare and industrial automation. Let's examine the definitions, salient traits, and contemporary functions of embedded systems and IoT:

9.1.1. Embedded Systems:

An embedded system is a specialized computing device or microcontroller-based system created to carry out particular activities or functions as part of a larger system. In order to effectively perform preset operations, these systems are firmly integrated into hardware and software.

9.1.2. Important Characteristics:

a. **Specialized Functionality:** Embedded systems are designed to do certain jobs, such managing sensors, operating machinery, or processing data in real time.
b. **Real-Time Operation:** A lot of embedded systems need to react to inputs or events in real-time or very close to real-time.
c. **Resource Constraints**: Compared to general-purpose computers, embedded systems frequently have less computational capacity, memory, and storage.
d. **Dedicated Hardware:** They are generally built into hardware elements like microcontrollers or processors under the heading of "Dedicated Hardware."
e. **Reliability**: Because they are frequently employed in safety-critical applications, embedded systems are built for high reliability.
f. **Applications:** Embedded systems are used in a variety of

settings, such as:

- Home appliances, smart TVs, and other consumer electronics
- Informational systems and engine control units for automobiles
- Automation in industry (PLCs, robotics)
- (Pacemakers, Infusion Pumps) Medical devices
- Defence and aerospace (avionics, flight control systems)

9.1.3. IoT: "Internet of Things"

The Internet of Things (IoT) is a network of connected machines, furnishings, and sensors that can talk to one another and share data online. By connecting embedded devices to the internet, IoT expands their capabilities by enabling remote data analysis, control, and monitoring.

9.1.4. Important Characteristics:

a. **Connectivity:** IoT devices have connectivity, allowing for remote access and control through the internet or private networks.
b. **Data Exchange**: IoT devices gather and send data to centralized systems or other devices, frequently in real time, for analysis and decision-making.
c. **Scalability**: From a few to billion devices, IoT networks can scale to support a sizable number of them.
d. **Diverse Applications:** IoT has a wide range of applications, including those in smart cities, agriculture, healthcare, and transportation.
e. **Data analytics and machine learning** are essential for gaining insights and improving operations since IoT generates vast volumes of data.
f. **Applications:** There are many different IoT applications,

such as:

1. **(Smart thermostats, security cameras) Smart home automation**
2. **Monitoring and streamlining manufacturing operations using industrial IoT**
3. **Healthcare (wearable health gadgets, remote patient monitoring)**
4. **Agriculture (monitoring soil and crops, precision farming)**
5. **Intelligent cities (traffic and waste management)**

9.1.5. IoT and Embedded Systems: A Relationship

- IoT devices are built on embedded systems. Embedded hardware and software platforms are used in the construction of many IoT devices.
- By linking embedded systems to the internet, IoT expands their functionality by enabling data exchange, remote control, and centralized management.
- In Internet of Things applications, embedded systems frequently act as sensors, actuators, or controllers. A temperature sensor, for instance, is an embedded system component in a smart thermostat.
- IoT and embedded systems work together to provide intelligent, interconnected solutions that improve productivity, convenience, and automation across a range of industries.

Both embedded systems and the Internet of Things (IoT) are essential elements of contemporary technological ecosystems and have been instrumental in the creation of intelligent, networked products and systems. The potential for breakthroughs in industries including automation, healthcare, energy efficiency, and environmental monitoring is enormous as a result of their ongoing development and integration into daily life.

9.2. Basics of Embedded Systems

The purpose of embedded systems is to carry out specific activities or functions within a broader system. They are a crucial component of many everyday objects and systems, from consumer electronics and domestic appliances to industrial equipment and automobile systems. Basics of embedded systems are as follows:

9.2.1. Definition

A hardware and software combination called an embedded system is created to carry out particular tasks or activities. It is "embedded" into a bigger system or gadget, frequently with real-time or almost real-time demands.

9.2.2. Important Features:

a. **Dedicated Functionality**: Software on embedded systems is developed specifically to carry out the duties for which they were designed.
b. **Real-Time Operation**: A lot of embedded systems need to react quickly or in real-time to inputs from the outside world.
c. **Resource Constraints**: Compared to general-purpose computers, they often have less computational power, memory, storage, and energy resources.
d. **Integration:** Embedded systems frequently make use of microcontrollers or microprocessors to tightly integrate with the hardware they manage.
e. **Reliability:** High reliability is an essential requirement for many embedded systems, particularly in applications that are safety-critical.

9.2.3. A System's Embedded Components

a. **Hardware:** Microcontrollers, microprocessors, sensors, actuators, memory, input/output interfaces, and power supply units are all considered to be part of the hardware of an embedded system.
b. **Software:** Embedded software is in charge of handling interactions with the external world, regulating the hardware, and carrying out specific duties. Low-level programming languages like C or assembly language are frequently used to create it.
c. **Firmware:** System booting and hardware initialization are handled by firmware, a type of software that is permanently stored in non-volatile memory (such as ROM or flash memory).

9.2.4. Uses for Embedded Systems

a. Embedded systems are commonplace and employed in a variety of applications, such as:
    i. Including smartphones, smart TVs, and washing machines, consumer electronics
    ii. Informational systems and engine control units for automobiles
    iii. Automation in industry (PLCs, robotics)
    iv. (Pacemakers, Infusion Pumps) Medical devices
    v. Defence and aerospace (avionics, flight control systems)
    vi. Smart thermostats and security cameras for the home

9.2.5. Programming and Development:

- Hardware design, software development, and integration are all necessary for developing embedded systems.

- Due to resource limitations, embedded software is frequently written in languages like C or assembly code.
- Integrated development environments (IDEs) and cross-compilers are frequently employed in the creation of embedded software.
- Testing and debugging are essential steps in ensuring the accuracy and dependability of embedded systems.

9.2.6. Difficulties and Things to Think About

- **Power Efficiency**: Since embedded systems sometimes run on battery power or are subject to stringent power limitations, power efficiency is of the utmost importance.
- **Requirements For Real-Time:** For many embedded systems, meeting real-time deadlines and response times is essential.
- **Security:** As embedded systems (such as Internet of Things devices) grow more interconnected, security concerns are crucial to ward off vulnerabilities and attacks.
- **Scalability:** Careful design is necessary since some embedded systems may need to scale in order to meet future requirements.

Modern technology relies heavily on embedded systems because they make it possible to automate and operate a wide variety of systems and devices. They have become an integral part of our daily lives as a result of their broad use, which continues to spur innovation across numerous industries.

9.3. Real-time Operating Systems

An RTOS is a specialized operating system created to satisfy the exacting timing and responsiveness demands of real-time systems and applications. Real-time systems are ones where prompt and consistent reactions to inputs from the outside world are essential. Numerous industries, such as industrial automation, automotive systems, healthcare, aerospace, and telecommunications use RTOSs.

The following are some essential qualities and traits of real-time operating systems:

9.3.1. Deterministic Response: An RTOS's predictable reaction time is its most important feature. It ensures that operations or tasks will be carried out within the allotted time limits, resulting in predictable and dependable system behaviour.

9.3.2. **Task Scheduling**: Task management and scheduling algorithms are used by RTOSs to manage tasks according to their priorities and deadlines. Pre-emptive priority scheduling, fixed-priority scheduling, and earliest deadline first (EDF) scheduling are frequently used scheduling techniques in RTOSs.

9.3.3. Task Priorities: In an RTOS, tasks are given priorities, which determine the order in which they are carried out. To achieve deadlines, higher-priority projects take precedence over lower-priority ones.

9.3.4. **Interrupt Handling**: To react fast and deterministically to outside events and hardware interrupts, RTOSs offer effective interrupt handling techniques.

Time-sensitive situations are frequently handled with interrupt service routines (ISRs).

9.3.5. **Minimal Latency:** The time that passes between an event occurring and the start of a response is known as latency, and RTOSs work to reduce this time. Real-time apps like must have low latency.

9.3.6. **Resource Administration**: Memory, CPU time, and I/O resources are all effectively managed by RTOSs. To avoid memory fragmentation and unpredictably long delays, memory allocation and deallocation are frequently deterministic processes.

9.3.7. **Mechanisms for Communication**: RTOSs offer communication channels so that tasks can synchronize their execution and communicate information. Shared memory, semaphores, and message queues are some of these methods.

9.3.8. **Services for timers**: Timer services are provided by RTOSs to schedule and initiate ongoing or sporadic tasks and events. Timers are necessary to manage time-sensitive tasks and routine updates.

9.3.9. **Handling Errors:** To detect and recover from problems without affecting the system's real-time performance, RTOSs frequently contain error handling and fault tolerance methods.

9.3.10. **Scalability:** Many RTOSs are built to be scalable, making it possible to create applications for a variety of resource limitations, from simple embedded devices to sophisticated multi-core CPUs.

9.3.11. **Safety and Certification:** To ensure they fulfil strict safety standards, RTOSs used in safety-critical applications, such as automotive or avionics, frequently go through certification processes.

9.3.12. **Portability:** Because RTOSs are frequently made to work across a variety of hardware platforms, it is simpler to create real-time applications that can be used on many embedded systems.

Among the most well-known RTOSs on the market are FreeRTOS, VxWorks, QNX, and RTEMS. The precise requirements of the application, the hardware platform, and the development tools available all play a role in the decision of which RTOS to use.

In conclusion, real-time operating systems are specifically designed to satisfy the stringent demands of real-time applications, where timing, predictability, and determinism are crucial. They offer a strong foundation for creating embedded systems and applications that must react dependably and quickly to inputs and events from the outside world.

9.4. Internet of Things (IoT) Concepts

The Internet of Things (IoT) is a technology paradigm that is rapidly expanding and transforming, allowing common objects and gadgets to be connected to the internet and gather, exchange, and act on data. IoT has several uses in a variety of sectors, including smart cities and homes, healthcare, and industrial automation.

Here are some basic Internet of Things concepts:

9.4.1. IoT Hardware: IoT devices are actual physical things or "things" that have sensors, actuators, and communication capacities. Examples include connected cars, wearable fitness trackers, smart thermostats, and industrial sensors.

9.4.2. **Actuators and Sensors:** Sensors are devices that gather information from the outside world. They can measure a variety of things, including temperature, humidity, motion, and light. Actuators are parts that can carry out tasks in response to commands. Switches, motors, and valves are a few examples.

9.4.3. Accessibility: Through a variety of communication technologies, including Wi-Fi, cellular networks, Bluetooth, Zigbee, LoRaWAN, and others, IoT devices are linked to the internet or private networks. Data transmission between devices and distant servers or other devices is made possible via connectivity.

9.4.4. **Information Gathering and Processing**: IoT devices' sensors continuously collect data. Environmental factors, user interactions, and device status may all be included in this data. Depending on the capabilities and requirements of the device, data processing may take place locally on the device or on the cloud.

9.4.5. **Cloud Computing**: The massive amounts of data produced by IoT devices are stored, analysed, and managed by many IoT solutions using cloud platforms. Scalable and affordable solutions for data processing and storage are provided by cloud services.

9.3.6. **Information Analysis**: The data produced by IoT devices is used to generate useful insights using data analytics tools and algorithms. This can involve trend analysis, anomaly identification, and predictive maintenance.

9.3.7. **Protocols for Connectivity:** IoT devices employ particular communication protocols to send data over networks in an effective and secure manner. MQTT, CoAP, HTTP, and AMQP are common protocols.

9.3.8. **Edge Computing**: In order to reduce latency and enhance real-time decision-making, edge computing refers to processing data locally on IoT devices or at the network edge (closer to the data source).

9.3.9. **Privacy and Security:** IoT security is essential for preventing assaults on networks, devices, and data. Encryption, authentication, and secure device management are security measures. IoT device data gathering and utilization raises privacy problems, necessitating adherence to laws and industry standards.

9.3.10. **Applications:** IoT applications are used in a variety of industries, such as linked cars, industrial automation (smart factories), precision farming, remote monitoring, wearable health devices, and smart homes (smart lighting, security systems).

9.3.11. **Smart Cities:** IoT is essential to the development of smart cities, which use data from sensors and gadgets to enhance public services, transportation, and infrastructure.

9.3.12. **Interoperability:** It is essential to make sure that IoT systems and devices can operate together without any problems. Interoperability is supported by standards and protocols from organizations like the Industrial Internet Consortium (IIC) and the Open Connectivity Foundation (OCF).

9.3.13. **Environmental Impact:** IoT can be used to monitor the environment and promote sustainability, including by managing water resources, checking air quality, and cutting energy use.

The Internet of Things is a rapidly developing technology that is anticipated to have a significant impact on a number of areas of our daily lives and enterprises. As the number of connected devices increases, it creates opportunity for automation, efficiency, and data-driven insights but also presents problems with security, privacy, and scalability.

9.5. Challenges and Opportunities in IoT

Significant prospects for innovation and efficiency gains across numerous industries are provided by the Internet of Things (IoT). To be widely used and successful, it must overcome a number of obstacles that it also presents.

The following are some major IoT issues and opportunities:

9.5.1. Challenges:

1. **Privacy and Security:**

- **Challenge**: Cyberattacks and data breaches may target IoT devices, jeopardizing data security and privacy.
- **Opportunity:** The chance to safeguard IoT ecosystems lies in the development of strong security standards, encryption, and secure device management systems.

1. **Scalability:**

- **Challenge:** Managing and growing IoT networks and platforms is becoming more difficult as the number of IoT devices increases exponentially.
- **Opportunity:** Creating scalable solutions for handling extensive deployments, such as edge computing and cloud services.

1. **Interoperability:**

- **Challenge:** The seamless integration of IoT devices and systems can be hampered by a lack of established communication protocols and compatibility.

- **Opportunity:** Using common IoT standards and protocols to assure compatibility and interoperability is an opportunity.

1. **Management of Data**

- **Challenge**: Managing the massive volumes of data that IoT devices produce can put a strain on storage and network resources.
- **Opportunity:** Using edge computing and data analytics to process data locally would eliminate the need for constant data transmission and centralized processing.

1. **Energy Efficient:**

- **Challenge:** IoT devices must run for extended periods of time without needing to replace batteries frequently.
- **Opportunity**: Designing energy-efficient Internet of Things (IoT) devices and utilizing low-power communication protocols to increase battery life.

1. **Regulatory Compliance:**

- **Challenge:** Data collection and transmission for IoT deployments frequently traverse international borders, necessitating adherence to various data protection and privacy laws.
- **Possibility:** Using data encryption and privacy controls to ensure that IoT systems abide by local and global regulatory requirements.

1. **Dependability and adaptability:**

- **Challenge:** Ensuring IoT system stability is crucial, especially in demanding applications like healthcare and factory automation.
- **Opportunity** to improve system reliability and resilience by implementing measures for fault tolerance, disaster recovery, and redundancy.

1. **Cost Restrictions:**

- **Challenge**: IoT device production, connectivity, and maintenance costs can be difficult to balance, especially for applications with strict budgets.
- **Opportunity**: Cost reductions may eventually result from economies of scale and technological advancements.

    1. **Opportunities:**

1. **Enhancements to Efficiency:** Businesses may boost productivity by optimizing operations, cutting operational costs, and better allocating resources thanks to IoT.
2. **Data-Driven Perspectives:** IoT creates enormous volumes of data that may be examined to yield insightful knowledge, improve decision-making, and develop fresh company strategies.
3. **Prevention-Based Maintenance:** IoT can be used for predictive maintenance to cut downtime and repair costs in sectors like manufacturing and transportation.
4. **Healthcare Innovations:** IoT makes it possible to remotely monitor patients, practice tailored therapy, and improve patient outcomes.
5. **Effect on the Environment**: IoT technologies can be applied to sustainable resource management, energy conservation, and environmental monitoring.
6. **The Smart City:** IoT can change urban infrastructure,

resulting in smarter cities with better waste management, transportation, and public services.

7. **Convenience for Consumers:** Voice-activated assistants, smart homes, and wearable fitness trackers are just a few examples of how IoT devices improve customer experiences.
8. **Opportunities for Innovation**: The Internet of Things (IoT) offers a platform for innovation, encouraging the creation of fresh goods, services, and business models.

In conclusion, IoT offers opportunities and difficulties across numerous sectors and applications. IoT may be successfully incorporated into our increasingly connected society by addressing security, privacy, scalability, and other concerns while using the promise for efficiency improvements, data insights, and innovation.

9.5.3. Key differences between Embedded Systems and the IoT

Aspect	Embedded Systems	Internet of Things (IoT)
Definition	**Embedded systems** are specialized computing systems with dedicated functions, often integrated into devices or appliances to control and monitor specific tasks.	**IoT** refers to a network of interconnected devices, objects, and systems that communicate and share data over the internet, enabling remote monitoring and control.
Connectivity	Embedded systems may or may not have connectivity features. They are typically designed for standalone operation.	IoT devices are inherently connected to the internet or other networks, enabling data sharing and remote access.
Purpose	Embedded systems focus on performing specific tasks or functions within a device or appliance, such as controlling a microwave oven or managing a car's engine.	IoT devices are part of a larger ecosystem that collects, shares, and processes data to enable smart applications and services.
Data Handling	Embedded systems may process data locally, and data is often used for immediate control or monitoring within the device itself.	IoT devices collect data, which is typically transmitted to cloud servers or other central systems for storage, analysis, and remote access.
Interaction with Users	Embedded systems may have limited or no user interfaces and are designed for specific, predefined tasks.	IoT devices often provide user interfaces or allow remote interaction through applications or web interfaces.
Network Connectivity	Embedded systems may support wired or local wireless connections, but they are not necessarily connected to the internet.	IoT devices rely on internet connectivity, often using protocols like Wi-Fi, cellular, Bluetooth, or Zigbee for communication.

Scalability	Embedded systems are generally standalone and not easily scalable or extendable beyond their original purpose.	IoT systems are designed to be scalable, allowing for the addition of new devices and services to the network.
Examples	• Microwave controller • Car engine management system • Digital thermostat	• Smart thermostats • Wearable fitness trackers • Connected home security cameras • Industrial sensor networks
Data Integration and Analytics	Embedded systems are not typically involved in data integration or advanced analytics.	IoT systems leverage data integration and analytics to provide insights, automation, and decision-making capabilities.
Security Considerations	Security may be limited to specific functions within the embedded system, with less focus on broader network security.	IoT places a strong emphasis on network security, authentication, encryption, and data privacy due to its internet connectivity.
Power and Resource Constraints	Embedded systems may have resource constraints but are optimized for specific tasks, often with low power consumption.	IoT devices may vary in resource constraints, but they must balance power consumption with the need for constant connectivity and data transfer.
Lifecycle and Maintenance	Embedded systems have a fixed purpose and may have a longer lifecycle but require	IoT devices may have shorter lifecycles due to rapid technological advancements,

maintenance or replacement when outdated.	requiring ongoing updates and maintenance.

Figure 18: Key differences between Embedded Systems and the IoT

Note: Embedded systems are specialized computing systems designed for specific tasks within devices, while IoT encompasses a broader ecosystem of interconnected devices with internet connectivity, enabling data sharing and remote access for various applications and services

Chapter 10: Advanced Computing Concepts

10.1. Introduction:

We will examine advanced computing ideas that have shaped and will continue to shape the discipline of computer science in this chapter. These ideas represent the most recent advancements in the field of computing and expand upon the fundamental ideas covered in preceding chapters. Among the major subjects covered in this chapter are:

The innovative field of quantum computing uses the laws of quantum mechanics to carry out computations at rates previously thought to be impractical using classical computers. The simultaneous existence of several states in quantum bits, or qubits, enables the parallel investigation of numerous solutions to challenging issues. We will examine the foundations of quantum computing and explore its potential uses in industries like drug development, optimization, and cryptography.

10.1.1. Artificial Intelligence and Machine Learning: Although AI and machine learning have already been covered in previous chapters, this section will go into greater detail about more complex subjects including deep learning, reinforcement learning, and generative adversarial networks (GANs). We'll look at how these methods are applied to develop intelligent systems that can perform functions like image recognition, natural language comprehension, and autonomous decision-making.

10.1.2. **Edge Computing**: Edge computing is a concept that reduces latency and improves real-time processing capabilities by moving computers closer to data sources. The purpose of edge computing, its architecture, and its uses in the IoT (Internet of

Things), autonomous driving, and smart cities will all be covered in this chapter.

10.1.3. Quantum Machine Learning (QML): Combines quantum computing and machine learning, promises the possibility of addressing complicated machine learning issues tenfold more quickly than traditional approaches. We will examine the operation of QML algorithms and their potential effects on different sectors.

10.1.4. Blockchain and Cryptocurrencies: Initially developed to support cryptocurrencies like Bitcoin, blockchain technology has now developed into a potent tool for safe and open record-keeping in a variety of fields. We will look at the core ideas of blockchain, its consensus methods, and it's more extensive uses outside of cryptocurrencies, including supply chain management, voting processes, and identity verification.

10.1.5. Neuromorphic Computing: The structure and operation of the human brain served as the inspiration for this method of computing. This section will discuss the possibilities for neuromorphic hardware and software to revolutionize cognitive computing and AI.

10.1.6. Supercomputing: At the vanguard of high-performance computing, supercomputers allow for simulations, research, and computations that were previously thought to be impractical. We will look at the architecture of supercomputers, their use in science, and how they affect areas like astrophysics, drug development, and weather forecasting.

10.1.7. Ethical Issues in Advanced Computing: As more potent technologies proliferate, ethical issues take on greater significance. This section will explore the moral conundrums raised by concepts in advanced computing, such as privacy issues with quantum computing and the moral ramifications of artificial intelligence and machine learning.

10.1.8. Future Trends: In the final section of the chapter, we'll look at some of the newest breakthroughs in high-tech computing, such as the creation of the quantum internet, advances in bioinformatics, and the fusion of AI and quantum computing.

You will have a firm grasp on these cutting-edge computing principles by the end of this chapter, as well as how they might influence technology and society in the future. These subjects are at the cutting edge of computer science, and because they are still developing, it is a fascinating and dynamic discipline for both academics and professionals.

10.2. Quantum Computing

The cutting-edge discipline of computer science known as quantum computing uses the concepts of quantum mechanics to carry out computations that are fundamentally different from those of conventional computing. Quantum bits, also known as qubits, have a property known as superposition that allows them to exist in several states at once, in contrast to classical bits, which can only represent a 0 or a 1. Due to its capacity to investigate numerous alternative solutions in parallel, quantum computers may be able to do some tasks exponentially faster.

The following are some essential ideas and features of quantum computing:

a. **Superpositions:** Qubits are capable of being in a superposition of states, which allows them to simultaneously represent 0 and 1. Quantum computers may do several calculations at once thanks to this characteristic.
b. **Entanglement:** Qubits can get entangled, which implies that even though they are physically separated by great distances, the state of one qubit is reliant on the state of another. Qubit processes can be highly coupled and synchronized thanks to entanglement.
c. **Quantum Gates:** Like classical logic gates, quantum gates are used to execute quantum computations. To carry out certain operations, quantum gates change the qubits' quantum states.
d. **Quantum Algorithms:** Unlike traditional algorithms, quantum algorithms use the features of the quantum world to solve problems more quickly. Shor's algorithm is a well-known illustration of how classical cryptography is in danger since it can factor big numbers exponentially faster

than the most well-known classical techniques.

e. **Quantum Error Correction**: External mistakes from noise and decoherence are quite likely to occur in quantum systems. The integrity of quantum calculations depends on quantum error correcting codes and methods.

f. **Quantum Hardware:** A number of businesses and academic centres are creating quantum computers. These devices can take many different shapes, such as topological qubits, trapped ion systems, and superconducting qubit-based quantum processors. To preserve quantum coherence, these systems are often operated at very low temperatures.

g. **Applications:** Quantum computing has the potential to revolutionize a number of industries, including cryptography (cracking and improving encryption techniques), optimization (solving challenging optimization problems), materials science (finding new materials with special properties), drug discovery (simulating molecular interactions), and artificial intelligence (accelerating machine learning algorithms).

h. **Challenges:** There are many issues with quantum computing, such as the requirement for error correction, the creation of scalable and fault-tolerant quantum hardware, and the effective conversion of conventional issues into quantum algorithms. Large-scale, useful quantum computers are still in their infancy and are not yet generally accessible.

i. **Ethical and Security Implications:** Quantum computing has ramifications for cryptography since it has the potential to compromise commonly used encryption techniques. Discussions about the necessity of post-quantum cryptography and the significance of data security in a quantum world have resulted from this.

j. **Quantum Supremacy:** When a quantum computer can do a task quicker than the most advanced classical computers, this is known as quantum supremacy. By completing a calculation that would have taken a classical supercomputer thousands of years to complete, Google claimed to have attained quantum supremacy in 2019.

Since the subject of quantum computing is still in its early stages of development, researchers are constantly trying to solve its problems and tap into its potential. One of the most intriguing and promising fields of computer science and technology, as it develops, it has the potential to bring about radical changes in many industries.

10.3. Neural Networks and Machine Learning

Artificial intelligence (AI) is made up of core elements like neural networks and machine learning, which have proven essential for resolving difficult issues in a variety of fields.

Let's delve more into these ideas:

10.3.1. Neural Networks

a. **Neurons and Layers**: Neural networks are computer models that draw inspiration from the human brain. They are made up of layers of neurons, which are interconnected nodes. Input, hidden, and output layers are the three most typical types of layers.

b. **Activation Functions:** Neurons apply activation functions to the data they receive as input, which causes the network to be non-linear. Among others, sigmoid, ReLU (Rectified Linear Unit), and tanh are often used activation functions.

c. **Forwardpropagation**: Data is transmitted through a feedforward neural network from the input layer to the output layer. Each layer's neurons process the input data before sending it to the one above them, and so on, until the final output is produced.

d. **Backpropagation:** When a neural network is trained, the weights and biases of the neurons are changed to reduce the discrepancy between the target values and the anticipated output. Using optimization algorithms like gradient descent, backpropagation is the act of sending mistakes backward through the network to change these parameters.

e. **Deep Learning:** Between the input and output layers of deep neural networks, also known as deep learning models, are several hidden layers. These networks have had outstanding success in a variety of AI applications, including image and speech recognition, and are capable of learning complicated hierarchical representations from data.

f. **CNNs, Or Convolutional Neural Networks:** Are specialized neural networks created for tasks like image and video analysis. They are effective at tasks like image classification, object identification, and image synthesis because they automatically learn features from raw pixel data using convolutional layers.
g. **Recurrent Neural Networks (RNNs):** RNNs are employed in speech and natural language processing, among other sequential data processing applications. They have feedback connections, which help them manage sequential dependencies and preserve internal memory.
h. **Long Short-Term Memory (LSTM) Networks and Gated Recurrent Units (GRUs)**: These specialized RNN architectures intended to solve the vanishing gradient problem and enhance the modelling of long-term relationships in sequential data.

10.3.2. Machine Learning:

a. **Supervised Learning:** In supervised learning, a dataset that has been labelled and contains input features and target labels for each data point is used to train the model. The model may forecast outcomes based on fresh, unforeseen data as it learns to map inputs to outputs.
b. **Unsupervised Learning:** To find patterns, structures, or correlations in unlabelled data, unsupervised learning involves training models on the unlabelled data. Common methods include dimensionality reduction (e.g., PCA) and clustering (e.g., K-means).

c. **Reinforcement Learning**: Reinforcement learning is a model in which agents develop their capacity for sequential decision-making by interaction with their surroundings. Depending on their activities, they are rewarded or penalized, and they try to maximize their total payout. This is frequently employed in robotics and game-playing applications.
d. **Semi-Supervised and Self-Supervised Learning:** Learning that is semi-supervised and self-supervised combines aspects of supervised and unsupervised learning. While self-supervised learning makes use of self-generated labels from the data itself, semi-supervised learning makes use of a smaller amount of labelled data and a greater amount of unlabelled data.
e. **Feature Engineering:** Is the process of choosing, modifying, or developing pertinent features from raw data in order to enhance the functionality of machine learning models. Some of this feature extraction can be automated using deep learning models.
f. **Evaluation Metrics:** Depending on the nature of the issue, several assessment measures are used to evaluate machine learning models. Accuracy, precision, recall, F1-score, mean squared error (MSE), and many more metrics are common measurements.
g. **Fairness and Prejudice**: Addressing fairness and prejudice in machine learning is a crucial ethical issue. Biases contained in training data might be inherited by models, resulting in unfair or biased results. Methods for identifying and reducing bias in AI systems are being developed by researchers and practitioners.
h. **Transfer Learning**: Transfer learning entails modifying previously learned models to perform certain tasks. This

method has become common in computer vision and natural language processing, where sizable pre-trained models (such BERT, GPT-3) are customized for different uses.

Numerous industries, such as natural language processing, image and video analysis, autonomous systems, recommendation systems, healthcare, finance, and more, use machine learning and neural networks. These domains are anticipated to become more integral to our daily lives and the resolution of challenging real-world challenges as they continue to develop.

10.3.3. Key differences between Artificial Intelligence and Machine Learning

Aspect	Artificial Intelligence (AI)	Machine Learning (ML)
Definition	AI is a broader field of computer science that aims to create machines or systems capable of mimicking human intelligence, including reasoning, problem-solving, learning, and decision-making.	ML is a subfield of AI that focuses on the development of algorithms and models that allow computers to learn and make predictions or decisions based on data.
Scope	AI encompasses a wide range of techniques, including rule-based systems, expert systems, natural language processing (NLP), robotics, and more.	ML specifically deals with algorithms that enable computers to learn from data and improve their performance on a specific task through experience.
Learning	AI systems may or may not involve learning from data. They can rely on rule-based logic, expert knowledge, or a combination of techniques.	ML is centered around the concept of learning from data, adapting to patterns, and making predictions or decisions based on that learning.
Human-like vs. Narrow AI	AI can be classified into two categories: narrow AI (or weak AI), which is specialized in specific tasks, and general AI (or strong AI), which possesses human-like intelligence and adaptability.	ML typically falls under the category of narrow AI, as it specializes in specific tasks and doesn't possess general human-like intelligence.
Data Dependency	AI systems may not be heavily dependent on large datasets for decision-making and can be rule-based or expert-driven.	ML heavily relies on data for training, and its performance improves with access to more relevant and diverse data.

Algorithm Development	AI may involve a broader range of algorithmic approaches, including rule-based systems, knowledge graphs, symbolic reasoning, and more.	ML is primarily concerned with the development and deployment of machine learning algorithms, such as decision trees, neural networks, and support vector machines
Real-time Adaptability	AI systems may adapt in real-time or operate based on pre-defined rules, depending on the specific application.	ML models can adapt and improve over time as they receive more data and undergo training iterations.
Examples	• Chatbots and virtual assistants (e.g., Siri, Alexa) • Expert systems for medical diagnosis • Autonomous robots	• Predictive analytics in finance and marketing • Image and speech recognition systems • Recommender systems in e-commerce
Problem Types	AI can address a wide variety of problems, including those that require symbolic reasoning, natural language understanding, planning, and decision-making.	ML is best suited for problems involving pattern recognition, classification, regression, clustering, and recommendation.
Generalization	AI systems may or may not generalize well across different tasks and domains, as they may be specialized in particular areas.	ML models are designed to generalize from training data to make predictions or decisions on unseen data, making them versatile in

		various applications.
Interpretability	Some AI systems, such as rule-based expert systems, may offer high interpretability, allowing users to understand their decision-making processes.	ML models, especially deep neural networks, can be challenging to interpret, leading to the development of techniques for model explainability.

Figure 19: Key differences between Artificial Intelligence and Machine Learning

Note: AI is a broader field encompassing various techniques and approaches to create intelligent systems, whereas ML is a subfield of AI that focuses specifically on developing algorithms that can learn from data and make predictions or decisions based on that learning. ML is a subset of AI, and both fields play important roles in the development of intelligent applications and systems.

10.4. High-Performance Computing

High-Performance Computing (HPC) is the practice of solving complex problems or carrying out extensive simulations and computations at speeds that are much faster than those possible with traditional computers. Since HPC systems are made to tackle activities requiring a lot of processing power, they are crucial in many fields of science, engineering, and research.

Aspects of high-performance computing include the following:

10.4.1. Parallel Processing: HPC systems rely on parallel processing, in which a number of processors or computer nodes cooperate to solve a problem at once. Complex tasks can be completed much more quickly thanks to this parallelism than they could be on a single processor.

10.4.2. **Supercomputers:** The most potent and well-known HPC systems are supercomputers. They are made up of thousands, perhaps even millions, of processors connected by quick networks. Supercomputers like IBM's Summit, Cray's Shasta, and Fujitsu's Fugaku are examples.

10.4.3. Clusters: To create a single, high-performance cluster, numerous regular PCs or servers are linked together. Cluster computing is affordable and popular in both industry and research.

10.4.4. GPU Acceleration: Graphics Processing Units (GPUs) have become more well-liked in HPC as a result of their effectiveness in handling parallel processing tasks. Deep learning, data analysis, and scientific modelling are frequently performed on GPUs.

10.4.5. Distributed Computing: HPC systems can be set up in many places, enabling organizations and researchers to use shared computing resources. Distributed computing is used by initiatives like SETI@home and Folding@home to tap into the processing power of volunteers' machines throughout the world.

10.4.6. Applications: High-performance computing (HPC) is employed in a variety of disciplines, including astrophysics, computational chemistry, molecular biology, nuclear simulations, financial modelling, and more. Previously unstudied complicated phenomena can now be simulated and analysed by researchers.

10.4.7. High-Performance Storage: To effectively handle massive datasets, HPC systems need quick and dependable storage options. For HPC environments, technologies like distributed storage systems and parallel file systems are crucial.

10.4.8. Software and Programming Models: Message Passing Interface (MPI) for interprocessor communication and OpenMP for shared-memory parallelism are two examples of specific programming models and libraries that are frequently used when creating software for HPC systems. These resources assist programmers in utilizing the power of parallelism effectively.

10.4.9. Scalability: A key component of HPC is scalability. To tackle bigger and more complicated problems, systems need to scale both in terms of computing power and data storage.

10.4.10. Energy Efficiency: Supercomputers use enormous amounts of energy, raising questions about their effects on the environment and their cost of operation. Through improvements in hardware and cooling methods, scientists and engineers are always attempting to make HPC systems more energy-efficient.

10.4.11. Obstacles: HPC must overcome obstacles such as high hardware prices, high power usage, complex software development, and the lack of qualified personnel to fully utilize these systems' capabilities.

10.4.12. Exascale Computing: Seeks to achieve computing capability in the exaflop range (a quintillion floating-point operations per second), is the next step in HPC. Exascale initiatives are being actively worked on by a number of nations and groups to address difficult global concerns.

Thus, for the advancement of engineering, technology, and scientific inquiry, high-performance computing is crucial. HPC will continue to be a crucial tool for addressing some of the most challenging and important issues facing the globe as computing needs in numerous fields continue to rise.

10.5. Grid and Cluster Computing

For high-performance and distributed computing, there are two related but different paradigms: grid computing and cluster computing. With the help of these methods, computational resources can be used effectively across a number of devices or nodes.

An overview of grid and cluster computing is provided below:

10.5.1. Grid Computing:

a. **Resource Sharing:** The goal of grid computing is to build a virtualized, shared environment that enables users to access and use computer resources (such processing speed, storage capacity, and data) from geographically distributed locations as if they were a single, unified resource.
b. **Distributed and Heterogeneous:** Grids are dispersed and heterogeneous in nature because they frequently use a variety of hardware and software resources. These assets could be the property of several entities or groups.
c. **Middleware:** The software that offers a layer of abstraction and manages distributed resources is a key component of grid computing. Grid middleware aids in resource allocation and coordination.
d. **High Throughput:** Unlike high-performance computing, which focuses on maximizing the speed of individual computations, grids are often built for high-throughput computing, where numerous tasks are completed simultaneously.
e. **Applications:** Projects requiring access to massive computer and data resources, such as scientific research and data analysis, employ grid computing. Examples include climate modelling, drug discovery, and particle physics experiments (like the Large Hadron Collider).

f. **Security and Authentication:** Grids frequently deal with sensitive data, thus strong security measures and authentication systems are needed to guarantee data integrity and stop illegal access.

g. **Global Collaboration**: Grids make it possible for scholars and organizations to pool resources and work together on significant initiatives without being physically close to one another.

10.5.2. Cluster Computing:

a. **Tightly Coupled Nodes**: Cluster computing uses a collection of tightly coupled computing nodes, which are typically ordinary servers or workstations, connected to one another within a single location or data centre.

b. **Single Administrative Domain:** Unlike grids, clusters frequently fall under a single administrative domain, which makes resource management and security simpler.

c. **Homogeneous Hardware:** Homogeneous hardware, in which all nodes have similar configurations, is frequently used to build clusters, making them simpler to maintain and program.

d. **High-Performance Computing**: Cluster computing and HPC are frequently used interchangeably. For demanding processing jobs like simulations, scientific modelling, and rendering, clusters are built to provide great computational power.

e. **Message Passing:** A standard programming model for cluster computing called Message Passing Interface (MPI) enables nodes to effectively interact and coordinate their actions.

f. **Load Balancing**: Cluster systems frequently use load balancing methods to evenly divide computing jobs among nodes and ensure effective resource use.

g. **Examples of cluster computing** include the well-known Beowulf clusters. High-performance computing environments are often constructed utilizing open-source software and commodity hardware.

10.5.3. Comparison:

a. **Resource Distribution:** Grids distribute resources among many administrative regions and locations, whereas clusters pool resources inside a single administrative region or data centre.
b. **Hardware Diversity:** While clusters use homogeneous hardware, grids can accept varied hardware.
c. **Scope:** While clusters thrive at high-performance computing jobs within a single company, grids are built for large-scale distributed computing and data sharing.
d. **Middleware vs. MPI:** While clusters frequently use MPI for message passing and coordination, grids rely on middleware for resource management.

Grid or cluster computing should be chosen based on the particular needs of a project or organization. While some applications may benefit from grids' ability to share resources globally, others could need cluster computing's unrestricted computing capacity and low-latency communication.

10.5.4. Key differences between Grid Computing and Cluster Computing

Aspect	Grid Computing	Cluster Computing
Definition	**Grid computing** is a distributed computing paradigm that harnesses the power of geographically distributed and heterogeneous resources to solve complex computational problems.	**Cluster computing** is a parallel computing paradigm that connects multiple computers (nodes) in close proximity to work together on a specific task or application.
Resource Type	Grids typically involve a wide variety of resources, including computing nodes, storage, data repositories, and even specialized instruments or devices.	Clusters primarily consist of homogenous or similar computing nodes, often sharing a high-speed local network connection.
Geographic Distribution	Grids span geographically dispersed locations, which can include different organizations, institutions, or even countries, connected via the internet.	Clusters are typically located within a single data centre or facility, with nodes physically close to each other.
Management	Grid computing often requires complex middleware and scheduling systems to manage diverse resources and ensure efficient allocation.	Cluster computing is comparatively simpler to manage, with shared local resources and less complex scheduling requirements.
Heterogeneity	Grids are highly heterogeneous, with various types of hardware, operating systems, and software platforms connected to a common infrastructure.	Clusters are relatively homogeneous, consisting of similar hardware and software configurations to simplify management and compatibility
Communication	Grids rely on wide-area	Clusters leverage high-speed,

	network communication protocols, which can introduce higher latency due to longer network distances.	low-latency local area networks (LANs) for rapid inter-node communication.
Resource Allocation	Grids often involve dynamic resource allocation, where tasks are distributed across available resources based on resource availability and requirements.	Clusters use static or semi-static allocation methods, with tasks assigned to specific nodes within the cluster during system setup or configuration.
Typical Use Cases	Grid computing is suited for collaborative scientific research, large-scale data analysis, and applications that require access to distributed resources.	Cluster computing is ideal for high-performance computing (HPC) tasks, scientific simulations, and parallel processing applications that benefit from local resource sharing.
Fault Tolerance	Grids typically incorporate robust fault tolerance mechanisms to handle resource failures or unavailability across distributed sites.	Clusters often rely on hardware redundancy and failover mechanisms to minimize the impact of node failures within the local cluster.
Scalability	Grids can be highly scalable, but the management of a large number of distributed resources can be challenging.	Clusters are scalable to a certain extent, with the addition of more nodes, but scaling beyond a certain point may require complex interconnects and management.

Examples	• The European Grid Infrastructure (EGI) • The World Wide LHC Computing Grid (WLCG) for particle physics • Global collaboration in climate modelling	• Beowulf clusters for scientific computing • Hadoop clusters for big data processing • Kubernetes clusters for container orchestration

Copyright: Patrick Mukosha (2023)

Figure 20: Key differences between Grid Computing and Cluster Computing

Note: Grid Computing and Cluster Computing are two distinct paradigms for harnessing computational resources. Grids focus on connecting geographically dispersed, heterogeneous resources for collaborative research, while clusters concentrate on creating high-performance, closely-knit environments for parallel computing tasks within a single facility.

Chapter 11: Future Trends and Innovations

11.1. Introduction:

This chapter will examine some of the most fascinating upcoming developments and trends that are anticipated to have a significant impact on the future of computers and technology. These developments are at the leading edge of research and development, and they have the power to drastically alter a number of sectors and facets of our daily life.

A few of the major subjects covered in this chapter are listed below:

- **Advancements in Artificial Intelligence:** are anticipated, including developments in reinforcement learning, deep learning, and natural language processing. We'll look at how AI is being used in a variety of industries, such as finance, healthcare, and autonomous systems.
- **The Quantum Computing Revolution**: By tackling complicated problems tenfold more quickly than conventional computers, quantum computing promises to transform computing. We will talk about the development of practical quantum computers and how they might affect scientific simulations, optimization, and cryptography.
- **Edge Computing:** The development of edge computing is being fuelled by the proliferation of IoT devices and the demand for real-time processing. We'll examine how edge computing is changing the way data is processed and how it helps with projects like smart cities and driverless vehicles.
- **5G and Beyond:** The introduction of 5G networks has made wireless communication faster and more dependable. We'll look at how 5G might affect sectors including

telemedicine, autonomous driving, and augmented reality.

- **Advances in Biotechnology**: CRISPR gene editing, and synthetic biology are creating new opportunities for bioengineering, customized treatment, and the prevention of disease.
- **Augmented and Virtual Reality:** Virtual and augmented reality are rapidly developing technologies that have uses in gaming, instruction, training, and healthcare. We'll talk about how these technologies might alter how we engage with both digital information and the real world.
- **Blockchain Technology beyond Cryptocurrencies:** The application of blockchain technology is expanding beyond cryptocurrencies into fields including voting procedures, supply chain management, and identity verification. We'll look at the cutting-edge applications of blockchain across several industries.
- **Neuromorphic Computing**: The architecture of the human brain served as inspiration for neuromorphic computing, which has the potential to produce highly energy-efficient AI systems. We'll talk about the development of neuromorphic hardware and software.
- **Biocomputing and DNA Storage:** Researchers are investigating the use of biological molecules, such as DNA, for computation and data storage in Biocomputing. We'll look at the development and prospective uses of Biocomputing.
- **Space Exploration and Commercialization:** Missions to Mars, outposts on the moon, and the expansion of the space industry are all part of the future of space exploration. We'll examine the developments' underlying technology and breakthroughs.
- **Sustainability and Green Technologies:** As

environmental worries intensify, we'll look at developments in electric vehicles, sustainable agriculture, and circular economy strategies.

- **Ethical Considerations:** With regard to privacy, bias in AI, data security, and the appropriate application of developing technologies, the rapid speed of technological advancement creates significant ethical issues. We'll talk about the moral issues raised by these trends.
- **Education and Workforce Development**: Modernizing education and training is necessary to prepare the workforce for the future. We'll look at programs and tactics for advancing the knowledge required for cutting-edge technologies.

Readers will have learned about the exciting developments and trends that are transforming our world by the end of this chapter. Understanding these developments is essential for people, businesses, and society to successfully traverse the rapidly changing field of technology and science. These developments bring both opportunities and problems.

11.2. Edge Computing

A decentralized computing paradigm known as edge computing puts processing and data storage capabilities closer to the point of use. *Edge computing* distributes these resources to the "edge" of the network, closer to devices and sensors, in contrast to traditional cloud computing, which centralizes resources in data centres that are frequently distant from end users. This method is becoming more popular since it can offer low-latency, real-time processing for a variety of applications.

Aspects of edge computing to consider include:

a. **Low Latency:** Edge computing speeds up data processing and delivery. It is useful for applications demanding real-time answers because it reduces the amount of time data must travel to a distant data centre and back by processing data locally, close to the source.
b. **Distributed Architecture**: Edge computing systems are made up of a network of edge devices, such as servers, gateways, and Internet of Things (IoT) devices, that are placed close to the data source. Together, these nodes process data and reach judgments.
c. **IoT and Sensor Integration:** Edge computing and the Internet of Things (IoT) are closely related. The processing of this data locally at the edge lowers the need to transfer it all to the cloud, saving bandwidth and enhancing responsiveness from IoT devices' massive data generation.
d. **Use Cases:** Edge computing has uses in a range of industries, including augmented reality (AR), virtual reality (VR), autonomous cars, industrial automation, smart cities, healthcare (e.g., remote patient monitoring), retail (e.g., inventory management and tailored marketing), and smart

cities.

e. **Fog Computing**: An extension of edge computing known as "fog computing" adds a layer of intermediary computing nodes (called "fog nodes") between edge devices and the cloud. Fog nodes can offer more storage and compute power while still retaining low latency.
f. **Security:** By processing sensitive data locally and limiting its exposure during transfer to the cloud, edge computing can improve security. Additionally, it enables quick security reactions at the perimeter in the event of threats or breaches.
g. **Scalability:** By adding additional edge nodes as needed, edge computing systems can expand flexibly to accommodate rising computational needs.
h. **Issues:** Coordinating and managing a distributed network of edge devices can be difficult. Careful design and management are necessary to provide data consistency, fault tolerance, and security across edge nodes.
i. **Hybrid Architectures**: Many businesses use hybrid architectures, which pair traditional cloud computing with edge computing. By processing data locally when necessary and employing cloud resources for global coordination, analytics, and storage, this strategy maximizes the benefits of both paradigms.
j. **Edge AI:** To enable intelligent decision-making at the edge, edge computing frequently combines artificial intelligence (AI) and machine learning (ML) algorithms. This is especially useful for autonomous car and sophisticated surveillance system applications.
k. **Standardization Work:** To ensure interoperability and security in edge computing, various industry groups and standards bodies are creating protocols and standards.

In a world increasingly dominated by IoT and smart devices, edge computing is a game-changing technology that responds to the growing demands for low-latency, real-time data processing. The ecosystem of edge devices and solutions is expected to have a significant impact on a variety of markets, including manufacturing, healthcare, transportation, and entertainment.

11.3. Augmented Reality (AR) and Virtual Reality (VR)

Virtual reality (VR) and augmented reality (AR) are immersive technologies that either completely virtualize an experience or combine it with the real world.

Despite certain similarities, they serve diverse functions and have unique qualities:

11.3.1. Augmented Reality (AR):

a. **Definition:** Augmented reality (AR) projects digital data—such as pictures, movies, or 3D models—atop the physical world. By supplementing what the user sees with digital content, it improves how the user perceives reality.
b. **Devices:** A variety of devices, including smartphones, tablets, smart glasses, and heads-up displays (HUDs), can be used to deliver augmented reality (AR) experiences.
c. **Interaction:** AR allows users to engage with the digital objects superimposed on the real world and is frequently interactive. Touch gestures, voice commands, or motion tracking may be used in this interaction.
d. **Applications:** These include games (such as Pokémon GO), navigation (such as AR navigation apps), education (such as interactive textbooks), and industrial use cases (such as maintenance and repair support).
e. **Examples of AR technologies** include the filters on Snapchat and Instagram, Google Maps AR navigation, and Microsoft HoloLens.
f. **Mixed Reality (MR):** A subset of augmented reality (AR) technologies, such as Microsoft's HoloLens, offers a type of mixed reality in which digital items are attached to and interact with the actual environment.

11.3.2. Virtual Reality (VR)

a. **Definition:** Virtual reality (VR) entirely isolates people in a virtual environment. Users typically interact with VR environments by donning a headgear that covers their field of vision and using hand controllers or other input devices.
b. **Devices:** VR headsets like the Oculus Rift, HTC Vive, and PlayStation VR are largely used to deliver VR experiences.
c. **Immense Experience:** VR strives to deliver an entirely immersive and frequently interactive experience. Users have the impression that they are in a computer-generated world, which may be wholly fictional or represent a realistic reality in simulation.
d. **Applications**: Include gaming, training (including medical and aviation simulators), education (including virtual field trips), therapy (including exposure therapy for phobias), and architectural visualization.
e. **Presence:** Virtual reality (VR) aims to give users the impression that they are physically present in the virtual world. A significant objective in VR development is to have a high sense of presence.
f. Simulator Sickness: If there is an imbalance between the visual and vestibular cues, certain users of VR may feel motion sickness or simulator sickness.

11.3.3. Comparison:

a. **Immersion Level:** While AR augments the actual environment with digital features without completely replacing it, VR offers a deeper level of immersion by isolating users from it.
b. **Interaction:** While interactive experiences can be supported by both AR and VR, VR often provides more

broad and immersive interaction options.

c. **Applications:** While VR is commonly connected to entertainment and simulation, AR is frequently employed for practical, real-world applications.
d. **Devices:** While VR generally relies on specialized headgear, AR may be enjoyed on a larger range of devices, including smartphones and smart glasses.
e. **Challenges:** While AR must deal with problems like object detection and alignment with the actual world, VR must contend with motion sickness and the requirement for expensive technology.

From gaming and entertainment to education, healthcare, and training, AR and VR both have the potential to revolutionize a number of different industries. Future interactions with digital information and virtual environments are likely to be influenced by their continuing growth and incorporation into daily life.

11.3.4. Key differences between Augmented Reality (AR) and Virtual Reality (VR)

Aspect	Augmented Reality (AR)	Virtual Reality (VR)
Definition	**AR** overlays digital content onto the real world, enhancing the user's perception of reality by blending virtual and real elements.	**VR** immerses users in a completely virtual environment, disconnecting them from the physical world.
Environment	AR is experienced within the user's existing physical environment, with digital elements added on top.	VR creates a fully immersive digital environment, isolating users from their physical surroundings.
Interaction	AR allows users to interact with both the real world and virtual objects, providing a mixed-reality experience.	VR users interact solely within the virtual environment, using specialized input devices or controllers.
Hardware	AR often uses devices like smartphones, tablets, smart glasses, or heads-up displays (HUDs) to project virtual elements onto the real world.	VR requires dedicated hardware, such as VR headsets (e.g., Oculus Rift, HTC Vive) and controllers for a complete experience.
Visual Experience	In AR, users maintain a view of the real world while digital elements are overlaid onto their field of vision, creating a "see-through" or "transparent" experience.	In VR, users are completely immersed in a virtual environment, with no view of the physical world.
Use Cases	AR is used for enhancing real-world experiences, including gaming, navigation, education, training, and industrial applications (e.g., maintenance and repair guidance).	VR is often used for immersive simulations, training, gaming, architectural visualization, and therapy (e.g., virtual exposure therapy).

Real-world Integration	AR integrates with and enhances real-world context, making it useful for tasks that require real-time interaction with physical surroundings.	VR is less integrated with the real world, making it better suited for scenarios where complete immersion is desired.
Presence	AR maintains a sense of presence in the real world, as users remain aware of their surroundings while interacting with digital content.	VR creates a sense of presence in a virtual environment, disconnecting users from the real world to varying degrees.
Motion Tracking	AR often relies on simpler motion tracking, like GPS, accelerometers, and gyroscopes, to determine the user's position and orientation	VR employs more sophisticated tracking systems, including external sensors or cameras, to provide precise positional and orientation tracking within the virtual space.
Mobility	AR is generally more mobile and can be experienced on a wide range of devices, including smartphones and lightweight smart glasses.	VR experiences often require users to stay in a fixed physical location and are less mobile due to the need for headsets and tracking equipment.
Examples	• Pokémon GO, which overlays Pokémon in the real world using smartphones • Smart glasses like Microsoft HoloLens for industrial applications	• Oculus Rift for immersive gaming • Virtual tours of architectural designs and simulations for pilot training

Figure 21: Key differences between Augmented Reality (AR) and Virtual Reality (VR)

Note: Augmented Reality (AR) enhances the real world by overlaying digital elements, allowing users to interact with both physical and virtual objects. Virtual Reality (VR), on the other hand, creates a fully immersive virtual environment, isolating users from the physical world for a complete virtual experience. Both technologies have unique use cases and hardware requirements based on their respective design principles.

11.4. Blockchain Technology

Blockchain technology is a distributed ledger that is decentralized and keeps track of transactions on numerous computers. It has drawn a lot of interest because it has the power to completely transform a number of industries by bringing security, transparency, and trust to online transactions.

Key characteristics of blockchain technology include:

11.4.1. **Decentralization:** Instead of being held on a single central server, data in a blockchain is distributed among a network of computers, or nodes. Due to its decentralized structure, the network is immune to censorship and single points of failure because no single entity has authority over the entire system.

11.4.2. **Distributed Ledger**: Because it keeps a continuously expanding list of records (blocks) linked together in a chronological order (chain), blockchain is frequently referred to as a distributed ledger. Transparency and redundancy are guaranteed since every member of the network owns a copy of the complete ledger.

11.4.3. **Cryptography**: Blockchain controls the generation of new cryptocurrency units and secures transactions using cryptographic techniques. Digital signatures and authentication are performed using public and private keys, which makes it very difficult to change or falsify transactions.

11.4.4. **Transparency:** All network users can see transactions that are recorded on a blockchain. Users' trust is increased by this transparency because they may independently verify transactions.

11.4.5. **Immutability:** A transaction that has been added to the blockchain cannot be changed or removed once it has been added. Consensus techniques and cryptographic hashing are used to accomplish this immutability.

11.4.6. **Consensus Mechanisms:** Blockchains rely on consensus processes to confirm and concur on the ledger's current state. Proof of Work (PoW), Proof of Stake (PoS), and variants like Delegated Proof of Stake (DPoS) are popular consensus methods.

11.4.7. **Smart Contracts:** Self-executing contracts with predetermined terms and conditions are known as smart contracts. They operate without the aid of middlemen when certain criteria are satisfied. Ethereum is a well-known blockchain that is used to implement smart contracts.

11.4.8. **Cryptocurrencies:** Bitcoin, which functions as a decentralized digital currency, was the first successful implementation of blockchain technology. Since then, a large number of additional cryptocurrencies have appeared, each with their own special features and use cases, including Ethereum, Litecoin, and Ripple.

11.4.9. **Applications beyond Cryptocurrencies:** Although cryptocurrencies are the most well-known use of blockchain, the technology has several uses outside of the financial sector. These encompass such things as data management for the healthcare industry, voting systems, identity verification, and more.

11.4.10. **Permissioned vs. Public Blockchains**: Blockchains can be classified as either private (permissioned) or public (open). Anyone can use public blockchains, which are maintained by a decentralized network of members. Private Blockchains give a group or organization more control over access and governance because they are only accessible to that group or organization.

11.4.11. **Challenges:** The scalability, energy consumption (in PoW-based blockchains), interoperability between various blockchain networks, and regulatory issues present obstacles for blockchain. For adoption to be more widespread, these issues must be resolved.

11.4.12. **Use Cases:** A number of sectors are currently investigating and implementing blockchain technology. Examples include keeping land records, validating academic qualifications, identifying the origin of food products in supply networks, and simplifying cross-border payments.

By offering safe, open, and effective solutions for a range of uses, blockchain technology has the potential to upend established institutions. Future digital transactions and data management are anticipated to be shaped by its continuing development and industry integration.

11.5. Bioinformatics and Biocomputing

Interdisciplinary domains such as bioinformatics and Biocomputing use computational and informatics methods to analyse and interpret biological data, support biomedical research, and improve our comprehension of living systems.

An outline of these two closely connected fields is provided below:

11.5.1. Bioinformatics:

a. **Definition:** The application of computational and statistical methods to the gathering, examination, interpretation, and management of biological data is known as bioinformatics. It entails the analysis of biological data, including DNA, RNA, protein sequences, and structural information.
b. **Data Types:** Genomic (DNA sequencing and analysis), transcriptomic (gene expression patterns), proteomic (protein structure and function), and metabolomics (small molecule metabolites) are just a few of the biological data types that bioinformatics deals with.
c. **Applications:** The study of structural biology, comparative genomics, functional genomics, and the development of new drugs all benefit greatly from the use of bioinformatics. It facilitates the discovery of genes, regulatory components, and disease-related biomarkers.
d. **Tools and Databases:** To store and retrieve biological data for analysis, bioinformatics relies on specialized software tools, algorithms, and huge biological databases (such as GenBank, UniProt).
e. **Sequence Alignment:** One of the core jobs in bioinformatics is sequence alignment, which involves

comparing DNA, RNA, or protein sequences to find commonalities, discrepancies, and conserved areas.

f. **Phylogenetic:** Based on sequence data, bioinformatics techniques are used to build phylogenetic trees, which show the evolutionary relationships between various species or genes.
g. **Structural Bioinformatics:** Predicting the three-dimensional structures of proteins and researching their interactions with other molecules are the main objectives of the subfield of structural bioinformatics. Utilized are methods like protein docking and molecular modelling.
h. **Biological Networks:** To comprehend the functional connections between various biological entities, bioinformatics is used to investigate biological networks such as protein-protein interaction networks, metabolic pathways, and gene regulatory networks.
i. **Personalized Medicine**: Bioinformatics is used in personalized medicine to develop medications that are specifically suited to each patient by examining their genetic and molecular profiles.

11.5.2. Biocomputing:

a. **Definition:** The use of computers and computational tools for modelling and simulating biological processes as well as for biological data processing constitutes the broader topic of Biocomputing.
b. **Modelling and Simulation:** In order to simulate biological processes and systems, Biocomputing develops mathematical and computational models. Cellular processes, population dynamics, and ecological systems are examples of this.
c. **Synthetic Biology:** In synthetic biology, where researchers

create biological systems by designing and constructing DNA sequences, circuits, and animals, Biocomputing is a key component. The creation and analysis of synthetic constructs are aided by computational technologies.

d. **Systems Biology:** The interdisciplinary discipline of systems biology, which frequently employs computational modelling and simulations, tries to comprehend the behaviour of complex biological systems as a whole. Biocomputing is a contributor to this field.

e. **Quantitative Biology:** To formulate and resolve biological problems, Biocomputing connects biology and quantitative disciplines, such as mathematics, statistics, and computer science.

f. **Complex Systems:** Biocomputing is used to investigate complex biological systems, including as ecosystems, ecological systems, and the interactions between various species within an ecosystem.

g. **Applications:** Biocomputing has numerous uses, including understanding the dynamics of infectious illnesses, population genetics, ecological modelling, and drug development.

For improving our comprehension of biological systems, customized medicine, and the creation of biotechnological solutions to difficult biological problems, bioinformatics and Biocomputing are both crucial. As biological data collection methods and computer power develop, these domains keep evolving.

11.5.3. Key differences between Bioinformatics and Biocomputing

Aspect	Bioinformatics	Biocomputing
Definition	**Bioinformatics** is an interdisciplinary field that combines biology and computer science to analyze and interpret biological data, such as DNA sequences, protein structures, and genomics data.	**Biocomputing** is a subset of bioinformatics that specifically focuses on the development and application of computational techniques and models to solve biological and biomedical problems.
Scope	Bioinformatics encompasses a broad range of activities, including data storage, retrieval, analysis, and interpretation of biological data.	Biocomputing concentrates on the computational aspects of bioinformatics, emphasizing the development of algorithms and models for biological data analysis.
Data Types	Bioinformatics deals with various biological data types, including genomics, proteomics, transcriptomics, and structural biology data.	Biocomputing specifically addresses the computational challenges related to biological data, such as sequence alignment, structure prediction, and data mining.
Applications	Bioinformatics is used in biological research, drug discovery, comparative genomics, evolutionary biology, and personalized medicine, among others.	Biocomputing is primarily applied to solving computational and modeling challenges in biology, such as predicting protein structures, simulating biological processes, and analyzing large-scale biological datasets.
Tools and Software	Bioinformatics relies on a wide range of software and tools for data analysis and	Biocomputing involves developing specialized algorithms and software tools for solving

	interpretation, including sequence alignment software (e.g., BLAST), genome browsers, and statistical packages.	specific biological problems, often requiring expertise in computational biology and bioinformatics.
Data Management	Bioinformatics involves data management, storage, and retrieval solutions for handling massive biological datasets, often using databases and distributed computing resources.	Biocomputing is more focused on algorithm design and implementation to process and analyze biological data efficiently.
Education and Expertise	Bioinformatics typically requires a multidisciplinary approach, with practitioners having backgrounds in biology, biochemistry, and computer science.	Biocomputing often involves experts with strong computational skills and specialized knowledge in biology and bioinformatics.
Example Tasks	• Sequence alignment and comparison • Phylogenetic tree construction • Functional annotation of genes and proteins	• Protein structure prediction • Molecular dynamics simulations • Drug discovery through virtual screening
Data Integration	Bioinformatics integrates biological data from various sources and formats to facilitate comprehensive analysis.	Biocomputing focuses on developing computational models and algorithms, often integrating them into bioinformatics workflows.

Collaborations	Bioinformatics often involves collaboration between biologists, bioinformaticians, and computer scientists to address biological questions.	Biocomputing specialists work closely with researchers and biologists to develop computational solutions for specific biological challenges.

Copyright: Patrick Mukosha (2023)

Figure 22: Key differences between Bioinformatics and Biocomputing

Note: Bioinformatics is a multidisciplinary field encompassing the analysis and interpretation of biological data, while Biocomputing is a subset of bioinformatics that emphasizes the development and application of computational techniques and models to address specific computational challenges in biology. Both fields play critical roles in advancing our understanding of biology and its practical applications.

Chapter 12: Ethical and Societal Implications

12.1. Privacy Concerns in the Digital Age

The rapid development of digital technology and the pervasive collection, sharing, and analysis of personal data have made privacy issues in the digital age more and more important. These issues cover a range of facets of our life and online interactions.

The following are some important privacy concerns and issues:

12.1.1. Data Gathering and Monitoring:

- **Mass Surveillance:** Concerns about mass surveillance systems that track people's online activities, communications, and movements have been raised since government agencies and private organizations have access to enormous amounts of data.
- **Data Brokers:** Without the people's knowledge or agreement, data brokers acquire and sell personal information such as surfing patterns, purchasing habits, and demographic data.

12.1.2. Data Security:

- **Data Braches:** High-profile data breaches disclose sensitive information, including credit card numbers and personal information, leaving people open to fraud and identity theft.
- **Cyberattacks:** Organizations are the target of malicious actors who want to steal data, interfere with services, or hostage-take data using ransomware assaults.

12.1.3. Online Tracking and Profiling:

- **Cookies and Tracking:** Websites and marketers track user online activity using cookies and tracking technology to build comprehensive profiles that may be used for targeted advertising and content recommendations.
- **Algorithmic Bias:** When employed in decision-making procedures like credit scoring or hiring, algorithms may reflect prejudices found in the data they were trained on, which can result in discrimination.

12.1.4. Privacy laws and authorization:

- **Complex Policies:** It can be challenging for people to comprehend the ramifications of giving their data because privacy policies and terms of service agreements are sometimes lengthy, convoluted, and written in legalese.
- **Consent:** It might be difficult to obtain informed consent for data collection and processing since many users might not completely understand how their data will be used.

1. **IoT data and location:**

- **Geolocation Data:** Mobile devices and apps gather location data, which may expose people's whereabouts and daily routines and can be used for a variety of things.
- **Internet of Things (IoT):** Smart gadgets may gather and transmit data in homes and workplaces, which raises questions about data security and surveillance.

1. **Online behaviour and social media:**

- **Online Harassment**: Doxing, and the improper use of personal data to target specific individuals are privacy issues.
- **Content Exposure**: Users may unintentionally reveal critical information or expose their private content to audiences they didn't intend.

1. **Health Information And Genetic Data**

- **Healthcare Data:** Privacy and security issues regarding sensitive health information are brought up by the digitization of medical records and the use of health apps.
- **Genetic Information**: As genetic testing services gain in popularity, concerns regarding the privacy of genetic data and its possible application to discrimination and profiling have been raised.

1. **Ethics-Related Matters:**

- **Ethical Use of Data:** In addition to privacy issues, ethical use of data issues include the possibility of using data as a weapon, manipulating it, or disseminating false information.

1. **Frameworks for Regulation:**

- **Data Protection Laws:** To create standards for data collecting, processing, and individual rights, many nations have adopted data protection laws, such as the General Data Protection Regulation (GDPR) of the European Union.

In the digital age, addressing privacy issues necessitates a multidimensional strategy incorporating legislation, technology, education, and individual understanding. While governments and businesses are expected to follow data protection rules and encourage responsible data practices, users are urged to take proactive measures to protect their online privacy. In an increasingly data-driven world, finding a balance between using data for innovation and protecting people's privacy is a constant problem.

12.2. Digital Divide and Accessibility

The gap between individuals who have access to digital technology like the internet and computing devices and those who do not is referred to as the "digital divide." This gap can take many different forms and has important ramifications for people, communities, and society.

The following are some significant facets of accessibility and the digital divide:

12.2.1. **Access to Technology**

- **Internet Accessibility**: Many people do not have access to dependable and reasonably priced internet connections, particularly in rural or underdeveloped locations. This may restrict their access to online resources, possibilities for learning, and employment.
- **Computing Devices:** To participate in the digital world, you must own a computer, tablet, or smartphone. However, not everyone has access to these gadgets, especially in areas with low economic standing.

12.2.2. Learning and Education:

- **Online Education**: Especially during the COVID-19 pandemic, the digital gap can have a significant impact on students' access to online learning resources. Students who don't have access to technology or the internet may have an academic disadvantage.
- **Skills Development**: In the employment market, digital literacy skills are becoming more and more crucial. For people on the wrong side of the split, the digital divide can impede skill development and constrict economic

opportunities.

12.2.3. Inequalities in Income:

- **Online Job Opportunities**: A lot of job searches and applications are done online. People without internet connectivity may lose out on job opportunities.
- **Financial Services:** As digital banking and financial services spread, persons without access to internet banking may be left out.

1. **Healthcare Inequalities:**

- **Telemedicine**: Digital equipment and internet connectivity are required for access to telemedicine services. The digital divide may make it difficult for some people to obtain essential healthcare resources

1. **Social Integration**

- **Social Engagement:** The internet facilitates social engagement, and social isolation can result from exclusion from digital platforms, especially in older persons.
- **Civic Engagement**: Access to government services and online information is essential for civic engagement. Those without access to the internet can find it difficult to participate in political processes.

1. **Geographical Inequalities:**

- **Urban-Rural Divide**: Rural inhabitants' access to high-speed internet is frequently limited, which limits their economic potential and informational options.
- **Global Disparities:** No single nation is immune to the digital gap. Due to considerable differences in internet availability and usage around the world.

1. **Initiatives and Solutions:**

a. **Infrastructure Development:** To increase internet access, governments and NGOs are working to provide broadband infrastructure to underserved areas.
b. **Programs to Promote Digital Literacy:** To close the gap, it is crucial to implement initiatives to promote digital literacy and offer training.
c. **Affordable Devices**: There are initiatives underway to lower the cost of computing devices, particularly in developing nations.
d. **Public Libraries and Community Centres:** Frequently provide free internet connection and instruction in digital skills.
e. **Public Wi-Fi:** To improve inhabitants' access to the internet, some cities offer free public Wi-Fi in specific locations.

Collaboration between governmental entities, corporations, non-profit organizations, and local communities is necessary to tackle the complicated task of closing the digital gap and increasing accessibility to digital technology. In an increasingly digital world, closing this gap is crucial to ensuring that everyone has equitable access to chances for social inclusion, economic advancement, and education.

12.3. Environmental Impact of Computer Systems

Energy use, electronic waste (e-waste), and carbon emissions are the main environmental effects of computer systems and the larger information technology (IT) sector. For the development of more environmentally friendly technological processes, understanding these environmental issues is crucial.

The following are some significant characteristics of how computer systems affect the environment:

12.3.1. Consumption of Energy:

a. **Data Centres:** Are significant energy consumers since they hold a large number of servers and computing devices. For power, cooling, and preserving ideal working conditions, they need energy.
b. **High-Performance Computing (HPC):** Because of their powerful processing capacity and intensive cooling needs, supercomputers and HPC clusters use enormous quantities of energy.
c. **Personal Gadgets**: Although personal computers, laptops, and smartphones have improved over time in terms of energy efficiency, the sheer quantity of these devices in use globally has not.

1. **Carbon Emissions**

a. **Energy Source:** The type of electricity utilized affects the carbon footprint of computer systems. The usage of fossil fuels in data centres and computing facilities increases greenhouse gas emissions.
b. **Manufacturing:** Carbon emissions are produced

throughout the production of computer hardware, including semiconductor fabrication and component manufacturing.

1. **Electronic Waste (E-Waste)**

a. **Hardware**: Hardware that is no longer in use: As technology advances quickly, obsolete computer hardware is discarded. If not correctly treated, dangerous compounds found in e-waste, such as heavy metals and flame retardants, can harm both the environment and people's health.
b. **Recycling:** To reduce the impact of e-waste on the environment, proper recycling and disposal are necessary.

1. **Resources for Material:**

a. **Resource Extraction:** Materials including rare earth elements, metals, and minerals must be extracted in order to produce computer hardware. Processes like mining and extraction may have a negative impact on the environment.
b. **Sustainable Sourcing:** To lower the demand for raw materials, efforts are being made to source commodities more responsibly and recycle parts.

1. **Cooling Techniques:**

a. Data centres and other large-scale computer facilities need a sizable cooling infrastructure in order to maintain ideal operating temperatures. The amount of energy needed for cooling affects both the environment and overall energy utilization.

1. **Green Computing Techniques**

- **Energy Efficiency**: To lower energy usage, manufacturers and data centre operators are putting more of an emphasis on energy-efficient hardware and cooling solutions.

- **Virtualization:** Virtualization technologies make it possible to combine several virtual servers on a single physical server.
- **Sustainable Energy**: To lessen their carbon footprint, some data centres and tech corporations are switching to sustainable energy sources like solar and wind power.

1. **Certification and Regulation:**

- **Environmental Standards:** Institutions and governments are putting in place rules and guidelines for the IT sector's responsible e-waste management and energy efficiency.
- **Programs for Certification:** Numerous certification systems, including ENERGY STAR for computers and data centres, encourage the use of environmentally friendly and energy-efficient goods and procedures.

A mix of technology advancements, energy-efficient procedures, ethical manufacture and disposal, and the utilization of renewable energy sources are required to lessen the environmental impact of computer systems. Sustainable and environmentally friendly methods of computing are essential to reduce the environmental impact of the IT sector as it expands.

12.4. Responsible AI and Algorithmic Bias

The creation and implementation of artificial intelligence (AI) systems must take into account ethical AI and the need to eliminate algorithmic bias. These ideas seek to guarantee that AI technologies are moral, just, responsible, and advantageous to all users and society.

An overview of algorithmic bias and responsible AI is given below:

12.4.1. Responsible AI:

- **Definition:** Responsible AI is the ethical and responsible design, implementation, and application of artificial intelligence systems. It includes guidelines and tactics designed to reduce risks and maximize the advantages of AI technologies.

12.4.2. Primary Ideas:

- **Transparency:** AI systems should be open and unambiguous in their decision-making processes.
- **Fairness:** Regardless of a user's demographic features, AI systems should be created and educated to deliver fair and unbiased results.
- **Accountability:** The decisions and acts taken by AI systems should be held developers and organizations accountable.
- **Privacy:** AI systems should uphold data protection laws and respect user privacy.
- **Safety:** In order to protect people and the environment, AI systems should be created with safety in mind.

12.4.3. Ethics-Related Matters:

- **Ethical Aspects:** The ethical aspects of AI systems such as their propensity to propagate prejudices, infringe privacy, or have unforeseen repercussions, are taken into account in responsible AI.
- The use of AI for societal benefit is encouraged by ethical AI frameworks, which also link AI development with human values and ideals.

12.4.5. Human-Cantered Design

- The concept of "responsible AI" highlights the significance of building AI systems with the requirements and values of human users in mind.

12.4.6. Algorithmic Bias:

- Algorithmic bias is the systematic and unfair prejudice that appears in algorithmic results, according to its definition. It may be the result of inaccurate algorithms, skewed training data, or other factors.

12.4.7. Types of Bias:

- **Data Bias:** If training data is biased or has historical prejudices, bias may be introduced into AI systems.
- **Algorithmic Bias:** When an algorithm uses biased features to make decisions, it might introduce biases into the system.
- **Feedback Loops:** AI systems that learn from biased user interactions and data might aggravate bias by reinforcing stereotypes.
- Examples:
    - Bias in recruiting procedures that target particular racial or ethnic groups.

  - Algorithms for biased predictive policing that disproportionately target neighbourhoods of colour.
  - Prejudice in credit scoring algorithms that limits access to loans and financial services.

12.4.8. Mitigation and Fairness

- Through assuring fairness in AI decision-making, such as through debiasing data, reweighting training data, and auditing algorithms, algorithmic bias can be addressed.
- Bias is evaluated and reduced using fairness indicators including demographic parity and equal opportunity.

12.4.9. Bias Detection and Testing

- To find and measure bias in AI systems, thorough testing and evaluation are necessary.
- Developers and organizations can track and reduce prejudice over time with the use of bias audits and ongoing monitoring.

12.4.10. Algorithmic Bias Mitigation with Ethical AI:

- **Data That Is Inclusive and Diverse:** Using inclusive and diverse training data reduces bias.
- **Ethical Principles:** Adhering to ethical principles and rules while developing AI.
- **Raising awareness** of algorithmic bias concerns and their repercussions is known as "bias awareness."
- **Collaboration across Disciplines**: Including sociologists, ethicists, and specialists from a range of disciplines in the creation of AI.

- **Continuous Monitoring**: Continually checking for unexpected biases in AI systems used in practical applications.

To ensure that AI technologies advance fairness, justice, and social wellbeing, responsible AI and tackling algorithmic bias are ongoing endeavours that involve cooperation among AI developers, regulators, legislators, and civil society.

Appendix:

1. Glossary of Computer Systems Terminologies

Terminology	Meaning
Computer System	A combination of hardware and software components that work together to perform computing tasks.
Hardware	The physical components of a computer system, including the CPU, memory, storage devices, and input/output peripherals.
Software	Programs and instructions that tell a computer what to do. It includes operating systems, applications, and system software.
Central Processing Unit (CPU)	The brain of the computer, responsible for executing instructions and performing calculations.
Random Access Memory (RAM)	Temporary memory used to store data and instructions that the CPU is currently processing.
Storage Device	Hardware components used to store data permanently, such as hard drives, solid-state drives (SSDs), and optical drives.
Operating System (OS)	System software that manages computer hardware, provides user interfaces, and runs applications.
Motherboard	The main circuit board of a computer, which houses the CPU, memory, and other components.
Input/Output (I/O)	The process of transferring data to and from a computer, often involving peripherals like keyboards, mice, and monitors.
Peripheral	An external device connected to a computer, such as a keyboard, mouse, printer, or monitor.
Graphical User Interface	A visual interface that allows users to interact with a computer using graphical elements like icons and

(GUI)	windows.
Basic Input/ Output System (BIOS)	Firmware that initializes hardware components during computer start-up.
Boot	The process of starting or restarting a computer, which involves loading the operating system into memory.
File System	The structure used to organize and store files on storage devices.
Software Application	A program designed to perform specific tasks or functions, such as word processors, web browsers, and games.
Desktop	The primary screen area where icons, shortcuts, and open windows are displayed.
Taskbar	A graphical user interface element that displays running applications and provides access to system functions.
Mouse	An input device used to move a cursor on the screen and interact with graphical elements.
Keyboard	An input device with keys used to input text and control the computer.
Internet Browser	A software application used to access and view web pages on the internet.
Firewall	A security system that monitors and controls incoming and outgoing network traffic to protect a computer or network.
Virus	Malicious software designed to infect and harm computer systems or steal data.
Malware	A broad term encompassing various types of malicious software, including viruses, spyware, and

	ransomware.
Ethernet	A network protocol used for wired network connections.
Wi-Fi	A wireless networking technology that allows devices to connect to a network without physical cables.
IP Address	A unique numerical label assigned to each device on a network for identification and communication.
Cloud Computing	The delivery of computing services (e.g., storage, processing, and software) over the internet, typically from remote servers.
Backup	Creating copies of data to protect against loss or corruption.
Algorithm	A step-by-step procedure or set of rules for solving a specific problem or performing a task.
Encryption	The process of converting data into a secure code to protect it from unauthorized access.

Figure 23: Glossary of computer system terminologies

Note: This glossary provides a foundational understanding of key computer system terms. Computers and technology continue to evolve, so staying informed about new terminologies and concepts is essential in the digital age.

2. Table of Figures (Key Differences between various Concepts)

Figure 1: Basic Diagram of a Computer

Figure 2: Key differences between Virtual Machines (VMs) and Emulators

Figure 3: List of differences between Von Neumann Architecture and the Harvard Architecture

Figure 4: Key differences between RISC and CISC

Figure 5: Key differences between HDD, SSD, Optical Drive, and Tape Drive

Figure 6: Key differences between Cloud Storage and Object Storage

Figure 7: Key differences between the TCP/IP model and the OSI model

Figure 8: Workstations in a Local Area Network (LAN)

Figure 9: Key differences between LAN and WAN

Figure 10: Key differences between Wireless Networking and Mobile Communication

Figure 11: Lists common Cyber-threats, how they attack computers, and mitigation strategies

Figure 12: The Key differences between Authorization and Authentication

Figure 13: Key differences between Encryption and Cryptography

Figure 14: Key Differences between Firewalls and Intrusion Detection Systems (IDS)

Figure 15: Key differences between System Performance and System Optimization

Figure 16: Key differences between Load Balancing and Scalability

Figure 17: Key differences between Caching and Data Access Optimization

Figure 18: Key differences between Embedded Systems and the IoT

Figure 19: Key differences between Artificial Intelligence and Machine Learning

Figure 20: Key differences between Grid Computing and Cluster Computing

Figure 21: Key differences between Augmented Reality (AR) and Virtual Reality (VR)

Figure 22: Key differences between Bioinformatics and Biocomputing

Figure 23: Glossary of computer system terminologies

3. Bibliography:

- *Anton, Howard (1987), Elementary Linear Algebra (5th ed.), New York: Wiley, ISBN[1] 0-471-84819-0[2]*
- *Bruce, Kim B. (2002). Foundations of Object-oriented Languages: Types and Semantics[3]. MIT Press. ISBN[4] 978-0-262-02523-2[5].*
- *Butterfield, Andrew; Ngondi, Gerard E. (2016). A dictionary of computer science (7th ed.). Oxford, UK: Oxford University Press[6]. ISBN[7] 978-0-19-968897-5[8].*
- *Mukosha, Patrick (2023), Fortifying Digital Fortress: A Comprehensive Guide to Information Systems Security, ISBN 9798223335160,*
- *Mukosha, Patrick (2023), Unravelling Information Systems: Exploring the Core Concepts, ISBN 9798223630845*
- *Gamma; Helm; Johnson; Vlissides (1995). Design Patterns: Elements of Reusable Object-Oriented Software[9]. Addison Wesley. ISBN[10] 9780201633610[11].*
- *Knuth, Donald[12] (1998). Sorting and searching. The Art of*

1. *https://en.wikipedia.org/wiki/ISBN_(identifier)*
2. *https://en.wikipedia.org/wiki/Special:BookSources/0-471-84819-0*
3. *https://books.google.com/books?id=9NGWq3K1RwUC&pg=PA18*
4. *https://en.wikipedia.org/wiki/ISBN_(identifier)*
5. *https://en.wikipedia.org/wiki/Special:BookSources/978-0-262-02523-2*
6. *https://en.wikipedia.org/wiki/Oxford_University_Press*
7. *https://en.wikipedia.org/wiki/ISBN_(identifier)*
8. *https://en.wikipedia.org/wiki/Special:BookSources/978-0-19-968897-5*
9. *https://archive.org/details/designpatternsel00gamm*
10. *https://en.wikipedia.org/wiki/ISBN_(identifier)*
11. *https://en.wikipedia.org/wiki/Special:BookSources/9780201633610*
12. *https://en.wikipedia.org/wiki/Donald_Knuth*

Computer Programming[13]*. Vol. 3 (2nd ed.). Reading, MA: Addison-Wesley Professional. ISBN*[14] *978-0-201-89685-5*[15]*.*

- *Mitchell, Melanie (1996). An Introduction to Genetic Algorithms. Cambridge, MA: MIT Press. ISBN*[16] *9780585030944*[17]*.*
- *Russell, Stuart J.*[18]*; Norvig, Peter*[19] *(2003), Artificial Intelligence: A Modern Approach*[20] *(2nd ed.), Upper Saddle River, New Jersey: Prentice Hall, ISBN*[21] *0-13-790395-2*[22]
- *Russell, Stuart J.*[23]*; Norvig, Peter*[24] *(2009). Artificial Intelligence: A Modern Approach*[25] *(3rd ed.). Upper Saddle River, New Jersey: Prentice Hall. ISBN*[26] *978-0-13-604259-4*[27]*.*

---

13. *https://en.wikipedia.org/wiki/The_Art_of_Computer_Programming*
14. *https://en.wikipedia.org/wiki/ISBN_(identifier)*
15. *https://en.wikipedia.org/wiki/Special:BookSources/978-0-201-89685-5*
16. *https://en.wikipedia.org/wiki/ISBN_(identifier)*
17. *https://en.wikipedia.org/wiki/Special:BookSources/9780585030944*
18. *https://en.wikipedia.org/wiki/Stuart_J._Russell*
19. *https://en.wikipedia.org/wiki/Peter_Norvig*
20. *http://aima.cs.berkeley.edu/*
21. *https://en.wikipedia.org/wiki/ISBN_(identifier)*
22. *https://en.wikipedia.org/wiki/Special:BookSources/0-13-790395-2*
23. *https://en.wikipedia.org/wiki/Stuart_J._Russell*
24. *https://en.wikipedia.org/wiki/Peter_Norvig*
25. *https://en.wikipedia.org/wiki/Artificial_Intelligence:_A_Modern_Approach*
26. *https://en.wikipedia.org/wiki/ISBN_(identifier)*
27. *https://en.wikipedia.org/wiki/Special:BookSources/978-0-13-604259-4*

Did you love *"Exploring Computer Systems: From Fundamentals to Advanced Concepts"*? Then you should read *Fortifying Digital Fortress: A Comprehensive Guide to Information Systems Security*[28] by Patrick Mukosha!

29

In our interconnected world, where information flows seamlessly across networks and systems, safeguarding digital assets has become an imperative. "Fortifying Digital Fortress: A Comprehensive Guide to Information Systems Security" is a comprehensive exploration of strategies, methodologies, and best practices that organizations and individuals can adopt to protect their information systems from ever-evolving cyber threats.

28. https://books2read.com/u/3nB809

29. https://books2read.com/u/3nB809

This book provides a holistic approach to information security, covering technical, operational, and human aspects to ensure a robust defence against cyberattacks.

About the Author

Patrick Mukosha is a Management Consultant originally from Kitwe, Copperbelt Province of Zambia. He has a Doctorate in Management (Strategic Management) and Masters (Strategic Planning) from Atlantic International University, USA. He also holds a bachelor's in Information Technology from University of East Anglia, Norwich, UK, and a Diploma in Business Management from Canterbury College of Technology, Canterbury, UK. Member of the Institute for Leadership Development, York University, USA (2001–08), He was elected Vice President-Midlands of Computer Society of Zambia (2004), Executive Director for VISION-2011 – a consortium of NGOs (2009 – 2011, Founder of Strategic Management Community of Zambia (2017), Vice Chairperson Mungule Ward Development Committee (2021-2026). He has worked for more than 15 years for International IT and Telecommunication companies in senior management portfolios. After finishing his PhD in 2017, he embarked on career as a Management Consultant. He has worked on several Strategic Planning projects and conducts coaching and mentorship in Entrepreneurship, Business Management, Strategic Management and ICT. He's an aggressive serial entrepreneur and founder of PatWest Technologies.

www.ingramcontent.com/pod-product-compliance
Lightning Source LLC
LaVergne TN
LVHW090309210926
848480LV00001B/190